Bill Davidson is a journalist and broadcaster of wide experience who has been described as one of America's best investigative reporters. Nearly five hundred of his magazine articles have been published and he has won all the top U.S. awards for magazine writing. Author of several other books, he spent six months working alongside the staff of the Los Angeles office of the Attorney General of California before writing *Indict and Convict*. He and his wife live in Connecticut.

Indict and Convict

Crime and Law Enforcement
in California: an inside story

BILL DAVIDSON

SPHERE BOOKS LIMITED
30/32 Gray's Inn Road, London WC1X 8JL

First published in Great Britain by Michael Joseph Ltd 1972

Published by Sphere Books 1975

TRADE
MARK

Set in Monotype Times

Printed in Great Britain by
Hazell Watson & Viney Ltd
Aylesbury, Bucks

ISBN 0 7221 2842 8

Once again to Muriel and Carol,
but also, this time,
to Davidson Matthew Pattiz

PREFACE

The Prosecutor. Reviled, unloved, unknown – except for the occasional Tom Dewey or Frank Hogan. On television and in fiction generally he's the ruthless Cromwell to the defense attorney's dashing King Charles. In the movies most often he's the plodding Watson to the superdetective Holmes. In the press: the F. Lee Baileys and the Edward Bennett Williamses outscore him ten to one in paragraph space.

In actuality, he's a human being comprised of the usual mixture of doubts, fears, and personal problems; and at his job he is capable of occasional foul-ups and occasional brilliance. Yet – though he and the legions of experts he commands are the cornerstone of the democratic American system of justice and law enforcement – what the prosecutor does and how he does it are almost totally unknown to the vast majority of the American public.

As a career-long investigative reporter, I became determined to observe a major prosecutor's office in action – from the inside. I selected the group portrayed in this book for two reasons. First, they operate statewide across the usually restrictive District Attorney's municipal or county boundaries, and the cases in which they become involved are much broader in scope and drama than the average DA's. Secondly, they gave me full, censorship-free cooperation.

For six months I worked out of a desk in their office. I had complete access to their files and memoranda, and I personally accompanied them into the courtroom and into the field – even, on one occasion, as a 'Special Assistant to the Attorney General.'

There is considerable dialogue in this book, which puts it in the category, I guess, of the recently christened 'nonfiction novel.' But all the dialogue is authentic. Much of it I heard and recorded on the scene. Other conversations were reconstructed after-the-fact by exhaustive interviews with the participants. A great deal is word-for-word from official tapes and transcripts – both from the Grand Jury and the Trial Courts.

The important thing is that all of the rather astonishing

events reported here are true, and all the people are real. The only dramatic license has been altering the chronology in some instances, and the only changes are in the names of undercover narcotics agents, to protect their identities, and the names of the unindicted and the unconvicted.

BILL DAVIDSON

CHAPTER ONE

It was dark in the living room of the ground-floor apartment at 185 Rivo Alto Canal in the Naples section of Long Beach, California, but the moonlight filtered in, reflecting streamer-like across the cluttered furniture, a lace-covered dining table set for two. It was the early morning hours of Saturday, April 8th, but the remains of the previous evening's steak, salad, and half-filled wineglasses had not been removed. Some light also seeped around a door, strangely set in a wall behind a couch.

Inside the bedroom beyond the door, a big two-hundred-pound man and an attractive red-haired woman lay side by side, her head on his shoulder, on a circular bed with a quilted and scalloped lavender-and-gold headboard and twelve brass-tipped wooden legs. The woman, in her early forties, was nude except for a black kimono with a gay white Oriental flower design, pushed up above her breasts. The man was fully clothed but with his trousers open.

Suddenly there was a muffled shot. A bullet creased the man's forehead and continued on through the skull of the woman, killing her instantly, and then burying itself in the quilting of the headboard.

Almost immediately a second bullet nicked the big man's ear and plunged into *his* skull.

After that, except for the labored, shallow breathing of the dying man in the round bed, now splattered with blood and bits of bone and brain tissue, there was silence in the apartment at 185 Rivo Alto Canal.

At 2.30 A.M. Frank Cornell, a commercial artist who lived in the apartment upstairs, heard two sharp sounds he thought might be shots.

At 4 A.M. another neighbor, named Charles Malaby, awakened in his apartment next door, at 189 Rivo Alto Canal. He decided to go to the bathroom, and as he stood there urinating, he looked out the window at the downstairs apartment directly opposite: number 185.

There was one light on – in the bedroom. Suddenly Malaby saw the bedroom light go out.

CHAPTER TWO

The events in Naples took place in the early morning hours of Saturday, April 8th. At 8:45 A.M. on the following Monday, April 10th, Tom McDonald, executive assistant to the Attorney General of California, was driving to work in his raffish, low-slung Morgan sports car. As he edged through the downtown Los Angeles traffic, McDonald, as raffish as his vehicle in gold shirt, paisley tie and neat curly red beard covering his otherwise boyish face, was startled to see a familiar figure futilely waving at taxicabs outside the Lo-Tel Motel.

McDonald eased over to the curb, opened the door, and said, 'Good morning, Charlie. Want a lift?' Charlie was Charles A. O'Brien, Chief Deputy Attorney General, the operational head of the AG's office and the number-two legal officer of the entire state. He did not become his lofty position now. He was sweaty and grumbling, his thinning hair askew, his usually pleasant Irish face with the pushed-in J. Edgar Hoover-type broken nose reflecting frustration and exasperation. As he lowered his athletic-looking forty-two-year-old six-foot frame into the tiny Morgan and finally came to rest with his legs stretched straight out in front of him, he growled to McDonald, 'Can't stay in a decent place in this goddam town, can't get a goddam taxi, and then I wrinkle my spine trying to get into this goddam scooter of yours.'

McDonald was used to the moods of O'Brien, his immediate boss, and he chose to ignore the insult to his car. Instead, he asked, 'Why *do* you stay in that motel with the traveling salesmen and the hillbilly tourists? If you were at the Biltmore where you belong, you wouldn't have any trouble getting a cab.'

O'Brien said, 'I stay at the Lo-Tel Motel because it only costs me ten dollars a night. The State of California sees fit to pay me the total sum of twenty-five dollars a day for travel expenses when I am not home in San Francisco. If I stayed at the Biltmore or the Hilton, the whole twenty-five dollars would go for the room and I wouldn't have enough money left to eat or even to buy a glass of wine. Besides, I know the owner of the Lo-Tel Motel and he gives me a big table to spread my papers out on.'

O'Brien thereupon lapsed into a brooding silence. McDonald, as he eased the Morgan through the heavy traffic of the Spring Street complex of courthouse and government buildings, reflected on the temporary frugality of his boss – a Harvard Law School graduate, friend of the Kennedys back in his native Massachusetts, a renowned gourmet, and possessor of nearly three thousand bottles of wine in his specially constructed dug-into-a-hillside wine cellar, possibly the finest in California.

They passed the glistening, glass-walled New State Office Building, and O'Brien growled, 'Why can't they put us in *there?* At least the air conditioning works.' McDonald thought of other things that didn't work in the new building, such as some of the more essential plumbing, but considered it better not to answer. He headed to the Old State Office Building diagonally across the street and pulled into the basement garage of the great granite WPA-Doric structure which houses the Attorney General's Office in Los Angeles. O'Brien worked here only two or three days a week. The rest of the time he spent in other offices of the Attorney General in San Francisco (his headquarters) and in Sacramento and San Diego. The Attorney General himself, Thomas C. Lynch, was in Los Angeles even more infrequently. It occurred to McDonald how both constantly complained that (a) most of the action seems to be in Los Angeles now, and (b) the building in which they have to contend with the action is inadequate.

The underground garage never failed to elicit a comment and O'Brien didn't disappoint McDonald this time. The garage was an afterthought, built many years later than the 1930's-vintage building itself, and O'Brien groaned as McDonald maneuvered the Morgan up and down the obstacle course of narrow winding ramps and massive concrete posts. McDonald finally reached his assigned parking place and they got out of the car. They trudged up one of the ramps and were nearly overrun by a party of C.I.I. agents (FBI-like investigators from the Attorney General's Bureau of

Criminal Identification and Investigation), coming down the ramp and carrying two or three submachine guns apiece. One of them raised a weapon in half-salute to the startled O'Brien and explained, 'We got these in a raid on the Minute Men, sir.' They were on their way to the arsenal, deep in the bowels of the garage.

O'Brien and McDonald puffed their way up another ramp and finally reached the elevators. They rose past five floors of warrens housing 120 lawyers and 50 investigators, all under O'Brien's control, and got off on the sixth floor. They went past a receptionist and into their offices, which adjoined each other except for a room in between for their secretaries, Dorothy Alexander and Muriel Duncan, both black. Before sitting down at his cluttered desk, O'Brien surveyed his office with distaste. The furniture, made by convicts in the California state prisons, was modern, with pale-green formica tops. The rug was beige. The wall decorations: an antique map of Mexico and a blown-up photo of a Los Angeles freeway at night. From the windows there was an unremarkable view of the Hall of Records across the street.

For O'Brien, as usual, the day's work consisted mostly of reviewing the progress of the hundreds of cases handled by the Attorney General's Los Angeles office. One after the other, teams of lawyers in the office would be led in by McDonald. They would tell O'Brien their problems, ask for his opinion about methods of procedure, or request his permission to do certain things that required his permission – such as wiring up a potential witness with a miniature radio transmitter for a meeting the witness was to have with a bribe-taking city official.

Habitually, the first to see O'Brien in the morning was Miles Rubin, the Senior Assistant Attorney General in charge of the Los Angeles office. Rubin, a suave, astute, transplanted young New Yorker with a black Thomas Dewey moustache, came in as scheduled and said, 'We may have something big cooking, Charlie, but I don't know enough about it yet. I'll see you later.' O'Brien, immersed in a draft of a new gun control bill the Attorney General was about to submit to the legislature, merely grunted. Rubin went out.

O'Brien spent the rest of the morning discussing with his

Deputy Attorneys General such matters as a state suit against an oil company for a ruptured gasoline line that was saturating the graves at Forest Lawn cemetery with high-octane fuel, an action against the city of Bakersfield for *de facto* segregation of its schools, a case against an out-of-state Mafioso named Jimmy (The Weasel) Fratianno who had moved in on the California trucking industry, an investigation of a bogus religion whose guru was living offshore on a heavily armed yacht, an inquiry into wholesale corruption and malfeasance in the San Diego police department, a suit alleging fraud in the computer dating industry, and a request to take action with the State Commission on Judicial Qualifications against a municipal court judge who had made anti-Mexican remarks from the bench. As was his custom, O'Brien conducted these discussions in a deceptively informal manner, meandering about the office as people haphazardly wandered in and out, perching himself on the edge of his desk or the conference table, even continuing to talk while making use of the facilities in his private bathroom.

By noon the office, now musty with cigarette and pipe smoke, had more or less emptied out and O'Brien asked McDonald if there was anything else. 'Yes,' said McDonald. 'Miles Rubin wants to talk to you, and there's Andrea Ordin, with the case against the door-to-door magazine salesmen.' 'Ah, Andrea,' said O'Brien, and he thought of his most attractive Deputy Attorney General, a striking-looking lissome young lady lawyer who used to be an actress and wore the most luscious of decorative mini-skirts. 'But,' O'Brien hastily added, 'Miles said he had something that might be important, so I better see him first.'

Rubin came in, his brown eyes snapping, his dark moustache twitching with excitement. 'What is it, Miles?' O'Brien asked.

Rubin said, 'Something we don't handle very often. Murder.'

O'Brien, who had been scraping the bowl of his pipe, paused with scraper in midair. 'Murder,' he said, 'is for district attorneys. Why not let Evelle Younger worry about it?'

'Not this time,' said Rubin, 'because one of Younger's own men is involved. It's Kirschke, Jack Kirschke. You know, the young Deputy DA in charge of the Downey office. He's the guy who worked so hard for Reagan in the last election and the rumor is that he's up for a judgeship. Anyway, his wife and another guy were found last night shot to death in bed. They'd been screwing.'

O'Brien said, 'I still don't understand why the DA can't handle it.'

'Because,' said Rubin, 'Kirschke himself is a suspect. He was picked up by the sheriffs in Victorville this morning. He was on his way back from Las Vegas. The DA probably is going to disqualify himself because it's one of his own men, and ask us to take over the case.'

O'Brien whistled. 'You better start from the beginning,' he said.

Rubin, who had launched his public career as an assistant prosecutor in New York City, was just beginning to warm up. He said, 'At this point, all we know is that a neighbor of the Kirschkes in Naples got suspicious because there were no lights in the apartment Saturday night so he lookedin the window late yesterday. He saw Mrs. Kirschke bare-assed and dead in bed, with a guy, also dead. The neighbor called the Long Beach police who found that both had been shot in the head, probably Friday night or early Saturday morning. The guy turned out to be a fellow name of Bill Drankhan who ran an aircraft-radio shop at the airport. Kirschke was away for the weekend at a Rotary convention in Vegas. It sounds to me like a pretty good alibi, but the police aren't sure, and when they couldn't find him, they ordered him to be brought in for questioning. That's why he was picked up in Victorville this morning. He was in his daughter's beat-up Volkswagen.'

O'Brien frowned. He said, 'Well, let's not get too excited. The alibi probably will stand up and the DA will be stuck with one more double murder to solve. Why don't you just keep in touch with the DA's office and let me know what's happening?'

Rubin and McDonald left and O'Brien went out to lunch. He enjoyed a filet of sole Véronique with the grapes just tart enough, and an excellent bottle of Batard Montrachet, 1964. He returned to his office to find Rubin waiting for him with Jack Goertzen, the chief of the Trials and Investigations

Section. Since Goertzen was then up to his ears in the prosecution of an errant tax assessor, O'Brien knew it had to be something important for Rubin to have torn him away from immediate work.

Goertzen said, 'Charlie, it's the Kirschke murder. Miles just got a call from Buck Compton.' O'Brien groaned because Compton was the Chief Deputy and troubleshooter in the office of Evelle Younger, the Los Angeles County District Attorney. 'What did Buck have to say?' he asked Rubin warily. Rubin replied, 'He said he didn't know what the evidence is but that if Kirschke is going to be prosecuted, we'll have to handle it. He said his office would assist us in any way they can.'

O'Brien sighed. 'O.K.,' he said, 'we'd better fill Tom in.' He placed a call to Thomas Lynch, the Attorney General, and the operator finally found the AG in his Sacramento office. O'Brien had Rubin and Goertzen give the details to Lynch and then he himself spoke to him briefly on the phone. When he hung up, O'Brien said, 'We're on the case, but it'll probably come to nothing, so let's not waste too much time on it.'

O'Brien was wrong. The Kirschke case was to occupy him and a good part of his staff for the next twelve months or more.

But then again, O'Brien was smart enough to realize that in his business he never really *knew* what events were going to shape his time and energies next week, next month, or even tomorrow. While he sat discussing the seemingly nebulous Kirschke case with his associates, for example, a series of widely scattered events were taking place in Southern California, all unknown to him at the time but all destined to end up on his desk, just as the Kirschke matter had.

In Palm Springs, California, a dapper young man in his thirties named Robert Drew Rand was making preparations for a party at his lavish $90,000 home, which he had bought from show-business personalities Tony Martin and Cyd Charisse. The preparations for the party involved ordering liquor, girls, and issuing instructions to his housekeeper-hostess, a handsome woman named Celia Gonzalez. All of the invited guests considered their host to be an heir of the Remington Rand family. None of them knew that he really was a Catholic priest, Father Robert Nikliborc, the administrator of a diocesan charity, Boys Town of the Desert.

In Encino, California, a middle-aged Hungarian refugee named Istvan Kovacs was working on a painting in his shabby little art studio. After every few daubs with his brush, he stepped back to admire his work. The work allegedly was an original Rembrandt called *Rabbi with a Turban*. There was another exactly like it on an easel about five feet away.

In Hollywood a handsome young man named Tom Devins was buying traveler's checks for a trip to Europe he was about to make. Devins was in the real estate business, and his traveling companion was to be an extremely wealthy woman named Mrs. Norma Carty Wilson, for whom he managed several buildings she owned. The blond, statuesque Mrs. Wilson was fifty-seven years old. Devins was twenty-eight. Previously he had been a parking lot attendant on the Sunset Strip.

In Santa Paula two muscular blond youths named Richard Ramsaier and Robert Verstraeten were teaching weight lifting to a group of kids in the local Boy's Club. The sponsors of the Boys' Club were unaware that both Ramsaier and Verstraeten were users and pushers of drugs. During a ten-minute break in their weight-lifting instruction, they had a quick whispered discussion about the sale of heroin, which they referred to by one of its street-names, 'shit.' Ramsaier said, 'There's only one way to make real money out of hustling shit. Them militants on the Santa Barbara campus and up in Oakland need guns. Anybody trading shit for hand-guns and machine guns and then selling them to the Commies and the niggers could make himself a fucking fortune.'

CHAPTER THREE

It was Wednesday, April 12th, two days after the Attorney General's office had taken over jurisdiction in the Kirschke murder case, but only a handful of people in the staid old building on Spring Street were devoting any thought to it. Instead, the bulky granite structure was humming with the everyday activity of its normal responsibilities.

On the ground floor, behind locked solid-oak doors, the chemist-agents of the department's Bureau of Narcotic Enforcement were cheerfully at work at their test tubes and microscopes, analyzing samples from about a ton of suspected marijuana and barbiturates seized from a plane downed in the Imperial Valley desert near the Mexican border.

On the second floor undercover narcotics agents of the BNE, as it's called, were writing up reports of their capture of the smuggling plane, which they had accomplished in a joint effort with aircraft of the U.S. Border Patrol. Most of the BNE agents were in their twenties and, appropriately, they sported long hair, sideburns, and moustaches, wore jeans, T-shirts, and other mod garb, better to blend into the drug-peddler environment they infiltrated daily. The young agents were, by law, all college graduates, and one of them, Roger Livingston, was studying for the bar at night. Another, Adam Greenbaum, had a master's degree in sociology and was the son of a prominent Southern California millionaire. Among the older men, who came into the bureau with at least five years of police department experience in the pre-college-degree-requirement days, was a burly and handsome Mexican-American named Sixto Ramirez. Ramirez was calmly counting out $13,000 in state funds at his desk. He was to use the money later in the day to 'make a buy' of a kilo or more of heroin from a major narcotics supplier, whom he had previously tantalized with smaller 'buys.'

On the third through seventh floors of the Old State Office Building, a small army of lawyers and C.I.I. agents were working on hundreds of cases that involved their specialities. The Civil Law Division was deep in the intricacies of the tidelands oil case and drawing up briefs to sue the Federal Government for issuing oil drilling licenses in the Santa Barbara Channel. The Criminal Law Division was busy representing the People of the State of Californa in all the appeals brought to the higher courts as the result of prosecutions by the state's fifty-eight district attorneys. The Division's lawyers were concerning themselves with everything from murder and sedition all the way down to fraud committed by a gypsy fortuneteller.

The Special Trials and Investigations Section was in the process of indicting a Los Angeles City Councilman for taking bribes to rezone a residential street corner for a gasoline station. The Consumer Fraud Section was assessing a fine against a swimming pool company which had agreed to stop phony advertising and to live up to the terms of its contracts with its customers.

In the Constitutional Rights Section an aggressive young attorney named Larry Tapper had convinced a judge to issue him a court order to remove the telephone of the National Socialist White People's Party in El Monte. The Nazis were playing a recorded 'kill-the-niggers' hate message over the phone in their headquarters, to anyone who dialed the advertised number. Tapper just then was instructing the Pacific Telephone Company to rip out the phone despite the protests of the seventeen-year-old Storm Leader who ran the Nazi headquarters.

In the basement dozens of machines were transmitting fingerprint information for local police to the Department's fingerprint file in the identification bureau and crime laboratory in Sacramento, second largest only to the FBI's in the entire United States. There also were requests for lie-detector experts, information about criminals with known methods cf operation, analysis of microscopic particles found in a suspected arson case, and biologists to confirm the findings of semen in a possible rape case.

On the seventh floor Andrea Ordin was looking over investigative reports in her computer-dating case, noting that one such service was charging up to $1,000 for electronic matchmaking and making only desultory use of its computer – if it used it at all.

On the fifth floor John Fiscus, the special investigator in the Charitable Trust Section, was scanning some routine reports from the Department's auditors in Sacramento. The Attorney General's office is required by law to supervise all charities in the state, in behalf of the poor and the voiceless, who otherwise would have no one looking out for their interests. Suddenly one return caught Fiscus's eye and a red warning light went off in his brain. The balance sheets just did not match up with the return of the year before. The return was from Boys Town of the Desert, Banning, California, Father Robert Nikliborc, Administrator. Fiscus made a note to himself to investigate the matter further.

On the sixth floor Chief Deputy Charles O'Brien was being interviewed in his office by a reporter who wanted to know if the California Attorney General's office, with all its powers to indict and convict, was unique in the United States. 'Bet your ass,' said O'Brien, who had been bored by the journalist's questions but whose enthusiasm now was rekindled. 'In every other state of the Union,' O'Brien explained, 'the Attorney General is largely a ceremonial figure with no powers and very little staff. Why did it happen differently here? It was a combination of the populism of Hiram Johnson and the genius of Earl Warren.'

The reporter was taken aback by the unexpected exuberance of O'Brien's reply, and O'Brien paused momentarily to savour the reaction since he knew the reporter had right-wing inclinations and disapproved of Chief Justice Warren's views after he ascended to the United States Supreme Court.

O'Brien went on to explain, 'When old Hiram Johnson became Governor of California in 1911, he rode in on a wave of populist sentiment which distrusted the power structure and wanted to return control of the state to the hands of the people. The power structure of that day was the Southern Pacific Railroad. They controlled *everything* – from banks to sheriffs to local political bosses. They committed unspeakable crimes against workers, farmers, and businessmen, but no one could touch the railroad because the railroad had the police and politicians in its pocket. It was old Hiram Johnson's notion that corruption always will be with us, so even after he smashed the power of the railroad, he pushed a bill through the legislature making the Attorney General the guardian of the guardians. He gave the AG's office the authority to indict and convict *anybody* – cops, sheriffs, mayors, even state officials. He wanted an independent presence, always looking around, crossing county lines, poking into everything. They called the AG's men "the headhunters" in those days, and I suppose there are still some who call us that.'

The reporter looked uncomfortable. 'But where did Earl Warren come in?' he asked.

O'Brien said, 'When Earl Warren was elected State Attorney General in 1939, he refined the process started by old Hiram Johnson. To give it more teeth, he built up the department into a replica of the Justice Department in Washington. He got topflight lawyers and organized them into divisions, and he got investigators as good if not better than the FBI. They began attacking crime and corruption where local sheriffs and prosecutors feared to tread. If you look in the files at your paper, you'll see newspaper pictures of Earl Warren leading boatloads of his men to close down the gambling ships that used to operate off the coast here.'

The reporter wanted to know why other states hadn't done the same. O'Brien said, 'New Jersey is planning to, and Connecticut and a couple of other states have bills in the legislature. They're all following the California model. Why, before he was assassinated, Bobby Kennedy told the Democratic Convention in New York that they *had* to create a strong Attorney General's office, just like the one in California. He said we don't have much Mafia activity here because the Mafia can't operate without local corruption, and the crooked sheriffs and cops can't be bought with *us* looking over their shoulders.' O'Brien chuckled. He said, 'I'll never forget the time we raided a sheriff's office up north. The old boy actually was running a string of whorehouses.'

The reporter asked, 'Is that why you moved in on the Kirschke murder case – because Jack is an Assistant District Attorney?'

O'Brien's chuckle abruptly faded. 'Yes,' he snapped, 'but I can't tell you anything about that right now.'

The reporter left and, vaguely troubled, O'Brien wandered into Tom McDonald's office next door. McDonald was settled in a leather easy chair behind his desk, his bearded face barely visible behind piles of newspapers stacked in front of him. O'Brien said, 'Anything from Miles Rubin on Kirschke?'

McDonald said, 'Yes, he's waiting to see you now.'

'Send him in,' O'Brien said.

A moment later Rubin slumped into O'Brien's office, his prosecutive ardor visibly diminished. 'We had to let Kirschke go,' he said. 'We didn't have any evidence to hold him longer than forty-eight hours. He's going to hold a press conference and go on television tonight. With all the publicity, he might get that judgeship yet.'

O'Brien said, 'I was in San Francisco yesterday. Bring me up-to-date on what happened since I saw you on Monday.'

In his precise way Rubin detailed how he had gone to the Long Beach Police Department headquarters with Keith Byram, supervising C.I.I. agent in the AG's Los Angeles office. Byram, a brash but talented young man who was about to take the bar exams to become an attorney, was appalled at the sloppy police work of the Long Beach police, who have jurisdiction in Naples, where the murders took place.

'There were footprints and fingerprints all over the place,' Rubin reported, 'and someone had removed the screen from the bedroom window. It may have been the murderer, and it may have been a curiosity seeker. No one seemed to know. Also, the photography of the crime scene was lousy. It all was in black-and-white instead of color so you can't tell blood from shadows. The photographer seemed to be more interested in crotch shots than anything else. After looking at all those pictures, we don't know too much about the trajectory of the bullets, but we know all about poor, dead Elaine's snatch.'

O'Brien groaned. 'Was that her name?' he asked.

Rubin replied, 'Yes, Elaine Terry Kirschke. She was a pretty well-known local dress designer. Worked for a guy named George Jacobs here in L.A., the firm name "George's Originals," but she once owned her own boutique under the name Elaine Terry. Not a bad-looking woman, forty-three years old. She earned twenty thousand a year. Kirschke makes eighteen thousand in the D.A.'s office, so between them they got nearly forty thousand a year, but they lived like pigs in that little apartment. All their money went into the Long Beach Yacht Club and a thirty-three-foot sloop they own. They were big entertainers, big drinkers. In fact, Elaine had. 18 per cent alcohol in her blood, which means she was pretty well tanked up when she was shot. There are two kids, a married daughter and a son, Doug, who's a senior at Colorado State.'

O'Brien asked, 'How about the guy who was killed in Elaine's sack?'

Rubin said, 'Drankhan, Orville W., nickname Bill, forty-one years old. He ran an aircraft radio repair shop at the Long Beach Airport. A big handsome guy, married, but with the reputation around town of being quite a cocksman. Hung out a lot at the yacht club bar, but never with his wife. He was a licensed airplane pilot. On Washington's Birthday he was arrested for drunken flying when he buzzed the yacht club. He had been giving Elaine flying lessons and she was with him in the plane at the time. But you want to know something funny? When Drankhan was arrested, Kirschke went down and bailed him out of jail, and then they all went to have a nice friendly cup of coffee.'

'Hmmm,' said O'Brien, 'tell me more about our friend Kirschke.'

Rubin said, 'He's forty-five years old, but looks younger. He's one of those handsome, slender cowboy types with no ass. He came here from Oklahoma as a boy and went to college and law school in L.A. and right into the DA's office, but he still pulls the turd-kicking act and keeps saying, "I'm just a little ole country boy from Oklahoma." He's been in charge of the Downey office for a few years now and has a good reputation as a tough prosecutor. A strong law-and-order man. Got a lot of good murder one convictions. The Long Beach cops like him. Captain Black down there told me he's held in high esteem by *all* the police in the area. They say he knew about his wife's playing around but he didn't seem to care. There are some rumours that Jack did a little nookie-chasing himself, but nobody has been able to prove it. The cops say nobody pays any attention to that sort of thing in that swinging, high-living yacht club crowd down at Naples.'

O'Brien said, 'I guess if you let Jack go, his alibi must look pretty good.'

Rubin said, 'The Long Beach police think so. Lieutenant Workman told the press that the case just isn't developed to the point where they could even get a complaint.'

'What's Kirschke's story?' O'Brien asked.

Rubin said, 'He told the cops he got home from work on Friday night – the night of the murder – and his wife was there. She made him a sandwich and helped him pack his seabag. He fancies himself a sailor, you know, so he doesn't carry a suitcase. He carries a seabag.

'He says he left the apartment in his daughter's Volkswagen and got to Los Angeles International Airport at 8:20 P.M., to fly to the Rotary convention in Las Vegas. He was too late for the Bonanza flight at 8:30 so he was put on standby for the 9:15 flight. When that was filled up and didn't take any standbys, he was told to wait for the Western Airlines flight at 11:30. At 11 P.M., he says, he decided to drive to Vegas in the VW. He says he stopped in San Bernardino for coffee and then, for gas, in Yermo, California, just outside of Barstow.

'He told the cops he got to Vegas at dawn, gambled for a while at the Desert Inn, and then went over to the Stardust to register for the convention. There's no question that he was there around breakfast-time on Saturday. He gave the cops the names of a lot of people he talked with and I have no doubt they'll back his story. He also says he thinks the gas station attendants in Yermo will back his story. If so, he couldn't have been anywhere near Naples when the murders were committed.'

'How so?' O'Brien asked.

'Because,' said Rubin, 'Elaine and Drankhan were seen leaving the yacht club bar together at about one A.M. A neighbor heard what he thought were shots at 2:30 A.M. Another neighbor saw the bedroom light go out at 4 A.M. If Kirschke was at the gas station in Yermo at 3:30 A.M., like he says, then he's clean. Yermo is at least a two-and-a-half-hour drive from Naples.'

O'Brien reflected for a moment. 'Just a couple of other

questions,' he said. 'I take it that Kirschke stayed at the convention until Monday morning when he started to drive home and was picked up by the sheriff in Victorville. What was his attitude when they told him his wife had been murdered in bed with another man?'

'That's a funny thing,' said Rubin. 'He was cool, very cool.'

'And what about the murder weapon?'

'The police can't find one. All they know from the ballistics tests so far is that the bullets come from a relatively rare pistol – a .38 caliber Harrington and Richards Defender. They used to be carried by the Federal Postal Inspectors years ago.'

O'Brien scratched his head. 'It's a funny thing,' he said, 'two high-powered lawyers like us and we're sitting here talking about guns and alibis like a couple of cops in the precinct house. Just tell me this. Do you think we have a case or not, so we can get back to more important matters like appeals to the United States Supreme Court?'

'It beats me,' said Rubin, his brow furrowed, 'but I think we ought to put some of our best investigators on the case to find out.'

'You do that,' said O'Brien, and he abruptly turned away to read a tidelands oil brief.

That night, while O'Brien was flying home to San Francisco to attend an American Conservatory Theater production with his wife, Marie, Jack Kirschke was interviewed on television. He was attractive and articulate.

He said, 'I have no idea who could have done this terrible thing. My best guess is that some embittered person I once convicted must have broken into my apartment and mistook Bill Drankhan for me.' He added, 'I can't tell you what it's like to be on the other side of the bars. It's something every law enforcement officer should experience.'

CHAPTER FOUR

On Friday an atypical heat wave – for April – assailed Los Angeles as the normally offshore winds shifted and began to blow in from the desert, in what is known as a Santa Ana Condition. The temperature rose into the high 90's, and there were mass mutterings in the Old State Building because the temperamental and elderly air conditioning system, unused to such early demands being made on it, refused to function properly. The Santa Ana Condition lasted for a full week. It did not help that it coincided with several developments that heated up, too, in the Attorney General's office.

On Friday morning Rubin, Goertzen, and a C.I.I. agent named Gene Frice drove to Long Beach for a face-to-face questioning of Jack Kirschke, which they had demanded. Kirschke, by now, had retained an attorney named Albert C. S. Ramsey, whose shrewd flamboyance in the courtroom, dramatic good looks, and gray-white hair prompted reporters of the Long Beach newspapers to refer to him as 'The Silver Fox.' Ramsey had opposed Kirschke many times in criminal cases, and they had considerable respect for each other. Ramsey had insisted that the questioning of Kirschke take place in his office.

It was a bad day all around for Rubin and the other AG men. When they arrived at the Silver Fox's den in Long Beach, they found the building swarming with reporters, who had been summoned by Ramsey. The press wanted to sit in on the interrogation, and television cameras already were cluttering the office. Rubin refused to permit this, and after much argument they settled down, *sans* press, in Ramsey's conference room. Also present were men from the Long Beach Police Department and from the Los Angeles County District Attorney's office.

Goertzen read Kirschke his constitutional rights, and then Kirschke, looking drawn but neither cocky nor subdued, launched into a narrative of the events of the murder weekend, telling essentially the same story he had given to the police. When he finished, Goertzen began the questioning. He asked about the Volkswagen. Kirschke said it belonged to his daughter who was married and pregnant back in Maryland. He said he used the VW for the Las Vegas trip because his own car, a Kharman-Ghia, was in bad shape after an accident.

Goertzen asked him about his relationship with Drankhan. Kirschke said he had met him only once, after he had bailed him out of jail for the Washington's Birthday drunken-flying incident. Kirschke said he only knew Elaine had been taking flying lessons with Drankhan and that he had no reason to suspect anything was going on. He added that he had no hostile feelings toward Drankhan or Elaine, with whom he had enjoyed normal husband-wife relations. At that point, after just two questions, Kirschke stood up and said, 'I'm sorry, gentlemen, but that will be all. I have to go to my wife's funeral.' He strode out of the room.

Outraged, Goertzen said, 'Stop him.' Rubin shrugged resignedly. 'We can't,' he said. 'All those reporters outside have to hear is that we kept a man from going to his own wife's funeral.'

They slipped out the back way to avoid the press. In the lobby Ramsey was briefing the reporters on what had taken place. He was quoted in that night's papers as saying, 'Mr. Kirschke is being badgered by the Attorney General.'

On Saturday and Sunday O'Brien rested. It was his fixed personal policy that no matter how hectic his Monday-to-Friday activity, he spent his weekends, whenever possible, with his wife and children. He was sitting in the living room of his home in Danville, about twenty-five miles east of San Francisco, staring through an all-glass wall at the incredibly beautiful vista of rolling green hills and grazing cattle, when the phone rang. It was Rubin.

O'Brien gloated momentarily about the heat wave he was escaping by being home in Northern California and then listened to Rubin's account of the fiasco of the day before at the Kirschke interrogation. To Rubin's surprise, the Chief Deputy was unexpectedly mellow about the news. In fact he even chuckled and said, 'Well, you have to admit it was a pretty good piece of stage-managing on their part. But don't try to compete with them in theatrics. Just get on with the investigation.'

O'Brien returned to the placidity he seemed to enjoy only at home. His wife, Marie, was in the kitchen making a particular favorite of his, the shellfish stew from the Italian Riviera called *cioppino;* and soon he would go out to his underground air-conditioned wine cellar, and from the thirty-six hundred bottles, all carefully filed away in racks by year and vineyard, he would select a Château Latour or perhaps even a Château Lafite Rothschild for his dinner. His three children, Devin, ten, Brennan, seven, and Erin, five, were playing noisily outside at the swimming pool.

O'Brien, a transplant from New England, enjoyed the California life immensely. Both he and his wife had been born and raised in Lawrence, Massachusetts, and he had followed Marie to the West Coast and married her after she had graduated from Radcliffe and emigrated to Los Angeles to teach. With his Harvard Law School degree, he first practiced law in San Francisco for six years, and then, bored by torts and contracts, he found himself drawn irresistibly to the more exiting life of the prosecutor. In his eleven years in the Attorney General's office, he had been Assistant AG in charge of the Criminal Division and was appointed Chief Deputy by the then Attorney General, Stanley Mosk, in 1961. Thomas Lynch reappointed him to the number-two job in 1964, despite his misgivings that sometimes O'Brien was *too* active a Chief Deputy. In one of the first peace demonstrations in Berkeley, for example, he had used karate chops he had learned in the Army to subdue a Hell's Angel motorcycle thug who was attempting to grind a lighted cigar into the face of a young girl student demonstrator.

Now O'Brien was considerably less vigorous in his prosecution of wrongdoers – physically, if not mentally.

The phone beside the Chief Deputy rang again. O'Brien recognized the clipped BBC accent as that of Eric Collins, a handsome six-foot-four-inch ex-British Army officer out of Sandhurst and the civil war in India, who was one of his best attorneys in the San Francisco office. 'Sorry to trouble you at home, old boy,' Collins said, 'but Andrea Ordin just called me with a couple of things from L.A. I thought you should know about.' O'Brien moaned. 'O.K., what are they?' he said.

'First of all,' said Collins, 'it seems that John Fiscus has uncovered a Catholic padre, name of Nikliborc, who's been doing some naughty things. Leading a double life in Las Vegas and Palm Springs while he's supposed to be running an orphanage called Boys Town of the Desert. All John knows so far is that the books of Boys Town are in a dreadful mess. You and Tom Lynch being Catholic, I didn't know whether it would be expedient for John to continue with the investigation. He's down in the desert, in Banning, now.'

'Goddam right it's expedient,' thundered O'Brien. 'What's your second problem?'

'A chap who's a television producer has donated a painting to the Bowers Museum in Santa Ana. It's supposed to be a priceless Rembrandt, a work called *Man in Armor*. Only there are some people at the museum who have questions about the authenticity of this masterpiece. They want us to use our crime lab to authenticate it.'

'But why *us?*' asked O'Brien.

'That's what Andrea said, too, but they insisted they're a public entity and they have a right to call on the state for help when they need it. They pointed out that the Santa Ana sheriff doesn't know much about art.'

'Oh, Lord,' said O'Brien, 'I guess we're going to have to become art experts. Tell Andrea to do what she can until I get there.'

On Monday, Tuesday, and Wednesday, O'Brien had his Los Angeles office organized for art research. Technicians from the crime lab in Sacramento shuttled back and forth to make chemical tests on the Rembrandt, and they grumbled about the commute because for once it was hotter in Los Angeles than in Sacramento. Andrea Ordin, abetted by a small army of other AG lawyers and C.I.I. agents, rushed about in the swelter trying to locate objective art experts. They were fortunate in getting two of the country's top Rembrandt authorities – Dr. Hans Huth, recently retired from the University of California, and Dr. Seymour Slive, Professor of Fine Art at Harvard University and curator of the Fogg Museum there.

Dr. Huth looked at the painting and snorted, 'This could not possibly be a genuine Rembrandt.' Dr. Slive was passing through Los Angeles on his way to Japan. Andrea set up a special room for him at Los Angeles International Airport, and she had *Man in Armor* brought there under special guard. Dr. Slive arrived from Boston, checked his schedule to make sure he had a couple of hours before his Japan Air Lines plane departed, and was escorted by Andrea to the examination room – a VIP lounge clogged with reporters.

Dr. Slive peered and poked at the painting. He stepped back, shook his head, and then examined it again – minutely. Finally he said, 'This is absurd. One of my youngest freshman students would know this is a fake.' He then left, exuding exasperation, for Tokyo.

The same afternoon, the chemical evidence came in from the crime lab in Sacramento. It was borne to O'Brien by Eric Collins. The first part of the lab report was easily understood by O'Brien. It stated simply that the painting was on a wood panel of a type never used by Rembrandt in any of his other works. The second part of the report was more complicated. It had to do with chemical analysis of the original pigments of the painting. The original pigments were buried under layers of paints used later in retouching, but the originals had been identified positively by the technicians through the use of electronic beams.

O'Brien muttered to Collins, 'Bureaucrats and scientists speak in elliptical Mandarin. What the hell does *this* mean?'

'Very simple,' said Collins loftily (he had had the advantage of a prior briefing). 'Rembrandt – full name Rembrandt Harmenszoon van Rijn – died in 1669. In the original pigments used by the artist who did this painting, our chaps have isolated three important colors. First of all, there's Scheele's Green, an arsenite of copper first discovered by the Swedish chemist Karl Wilhelm Scheele, who wasn't even *born* until 1742 – more than seventy years after Rembrandt was dead and buried. Then there's Prussian Blue, first discovered in 1704 – more than thirty years after Rembrandt's death. But the most flagrant of all is Emerald Green, which didn't appear until 1814 – more than a century and a half too late for *this* old master.'

'Oh,' was all O'Brien could say.

Thus fully armed with data, O'Brien immediately called a press conference, at which he tossed off Scheele and Slive and Emerald Green with insouciance, and officially declared the painting a fraud. He handled the physics and the chemistry masterfully, except for one mistake. He confused black light with ultra-violet light.

When the press conference was over, he asked Eric Collins and Andrea if they thought there was a cause of criminal action anywhere in the matter. Collins said, 'Unfortunately, no. The donor paid forty thousand dollars for the painting, which he bought from a Count Solito de Solis. The bill of sale claims no authentication. So that exonerates de Solis. However, I think we've opened a whole can of worms here which should be looked into. As you know, the Los Angeles *Times* already has run a series of articles about a wave of art frauds in California. We should do a full-scale investigation.'

O'Brien looked slyly at Collins. 'Do you know what *provenance* means?' he asked.

'Certainly,' said Collins. 'It's a French word used in the art world for authentication of the origins of a painting.'

'Okay,' said O'Brien. 'You're in charge of the investigation.'

By Thursday charitable trust investigator John Fiscus, poking around in the 120-degree heat of Banning and Palm Springs, had discovered that Father Nikliborc of Boys Town of the Desert and Robert Drew Rand, the Palm Springs–Las Vegas swinger, were one and the same man; that Nikliborc-Rand, with no provable source of income, had banked nearly a half million dollars in the previous nine years; that he owned the former Tony Martin–Cyd Charisse house in Palm Springs; that he had once owned an equally lavish spread in Las Vegas, which he had sold to a constant female companion of his, a pretty cocktail waitress named Nancy Brletic; and that he had sponsored, traveled with, and lavishly entertained a five-member girls' bowling team whose shirts bore the legend: 'Robert Rand, Palm Springs.'

On Friday morning Miles Rubin picked up the incidental intelligence from a friend in the District Attorney's office that a wealthy Los Angeles woman, Mrs. Norma Carty Wilson, had disappeared somewhere between Tangiers,

North Africa, and Geneva, Switzerland, while traveling with a young real estate promoter, Thomas Devins, who once was a parking lot attendant but who now managed buildings for Mrs. Wilson. The DA's man hinted mysteriously to Rubin that there might be a tie-in between this disappearance, a suspected murder, and a plot to free former Congolese premier Moise Tshombe, who was then imprisoned in Algeria.

On Friday afternoon Roger Livingston of the Bureau of Narcotic Enforcement met in a motel room in the city of Ventura, California, with an informant who always had passed reliable information to him in the past. Among the many titbits given Livingston by the informant, an addict, was an item that immediately caught Livingston's attention. 'There are two big dealers in smack, who don't want no bread, man, they only want pieces,' the junkie said. Translated, this meant to Livingston: 'Two heroin pushers are selling their wares for guns instead of money.'

'Where?' asked Livingston.

'Here, Santa Paula, Santa Barbara,' said the informant.

Livingston pulled out his notebook. 'The names?' he said.

'Dunno, man,' the addict said, 'I just hear them called "Squeak" and "Unk." '

'That may be enough,' said Livingston, closing his notebook.

At about 4 P.M. on Friday the week-long Southern Californian heat wave broke. The winds shifted around to their normal westerly direction and the damp air from the ocean brought a sodden fog bank rolling in from Santa Monica and northward along the coast. O'Brien gulped the mist happily as he rushed to the airport to catch a plane to attend a legislative meeting in Sacramento.

It was near the end of the session and the meeting didn't last very long, so O'Brien decided to drive back to his home in Danville, instead of taking another plane to San Francisco. He made the leisurely hour-and-a-half drive down Interstate 80, and while he was out of telephone contact, a tragedy occurred. His elder son, Devin, playing outside the O'Brien house, had slipped and fallen under a slowly moving milk truck. The rear wheel had passed over the ten-year-old's midsection.

O'Brien and Marie spent the next three days at the hospital until it was determined that Devin would live. The doctors could not say if the boy would be able to walk again or, if he did, whether or not he would be a eunuch, since his testicles had been crushed.

When there was nothing more O'Brien could do at the hospital, he went home, slept for a few hours, showered, shaved, and – knowing that his work was his best therapy – drove to his San Francisco office.

CHAPTER FIVE

The Attorney General, Thomas Lynch, was waiting for O'Brien.

Lynch is a tall, thin man with a lugubrious though ruggedly attractive face, who looks twenty years younger than his chronological age, which is the mid-sixties. He always dresses impeccably in a dark suit and tie, and his body always is lean from the hard work he does on his reconstructed old Monterey fishing boat, which, for relaxation, he frequently takes out into the Pacific with the commercial fishing fleets.

Lynch is the consummate politician. He built a strong electoral base from his own Irish background and the grandee flavor of his wife's Spanish Colonial heritage (she's an Estrada, one of the first Spanish families of California). This, added to a dogged and well-publicized fight against organized crime during three terms as District Attorney of San Francisco, made him an easy victor when he ran for Attorney General of California in 1966. He was the only Democrat to win state-wide office in what otherwise was a landslide victory for the Republicans, with Governor Ronald Reagan at the head of the ticket.

Now, as the highest elected Democratic official in the state, he led the party, practiced a policy of coexistence with Reagan, and worked closely with the Democratic leaders of the legislature. A gifted speaker and negotiator, he concentrated on the most public and the *least* public aspects of his office and left the day-to-day operations to his trusted Chief Deputy, O'Brien, although every major decision was made by Lynch and he knew everything that was going on in his sprawling organization. His relationship with O'Brien was a strange one – almost like that of a father toward a brilliant but impetuous son. Lynch was basically a conservative man in his concept of his office. He preferred mostly to act as lawyer for all the various state agencies which the Attorney General must, by law, represent in court. O'Brien, on the other hand, was more a proponent of the Hiram

Johnson–Earl Warren theory that the Attorney General's office must constantly attack, root out evil, indict and convict. Lynch, despite his misgivings, always had given O'Brien his head. It was much like their personal lives together. Lynch, although he knew good food, did not share O'Brien's extreme gourmet tastes in cuisine and wine. It was the same when O'Brien, who for years had lived just down the street from Lynch on Ashbury Place in San Francisco, decided to move out into the country. Lynch could not understand why anyone should want to abandon a great house in the middle of what he considered to be the greatest city in the world, but he shrugged and chalked it up to the differing tastes that make human beings interesting.

When O'Brien arrived at the office after his three-day vigil at the hospital, Lynch, knowing his Chief Deputy as well as Marie did, asked for only the briefest of reports on Devin's condition. Then, skillfully, he eased him into a discussion of what had been transpiring in the major cases in the office. O'Brien mostly listened, desultorily, until Lynch brought up the perplexing Kirschke-Drankhan murder. 'How's it going?' O'Brien asked.

'Badly,' said Lynch. 'To tell you the truth, I'm beginning to think we don't have a case against Kirschke at all. Evidence keeps turning up and then it pans out into nothing.' He filled O'Brien in on what had happened in his absence. First, Kirschke's own car, the Kharman-Ghia, had turned up in the airport parking lot. This opened up the interesting possibility that the assistant DA could have driven to Las Vegas early in the evening, flown back to Los Angeles International Airport, driven home in the Kharman-Ghia, murdered his wife and Drankhan, driven back to the airport in the Kharman-Ghia, and then had flown to Las Vegas again, where his alibi was established. But then it turned out that Kirschke had lent the Kharman-Ghia to an acquaintance named Donnie, who had left the car at the airport after the crime.

Next, a C.I.I. agent, Barney Allen, had located a Volkswagen of the same age and condition as the 1963 VW Kirschke had driven. Allen made the trip from Kirschke's apartment in Naples to Las Vegas in four hours and thirty minutes. On the same schedule this would have allowed

Kirschke ample time to commit the murders early Saturday morning and still get to Las Vegas by dawn. But this evidence was neutralized by the fact that a Kirschke-hired private detective, Joe Carroll, *also* acquired a 1963 VW and drove from Naples to the filling station in Yermo, California – where Kirschke maintained he had stopped for gas – in two hours and forty minutes. Carroll, moreover, had located two attendants at the gas station who said they remembered servicing Kirschke's beat-up Volkswagen between 3:30 and 4 A.M. the morning of the murders. The attendants were Dennis Baily, nineteen, and Gene Ledet, twenty-one. If their evidence stood up, Kirschke was in the clear. Frank Cornell, the Kirschke neighbor, had heard shots at 2:30 A.M. Yermo is 155 miles and two hours and forty minutes away. It was a physical impossibility for Kirschke to drive the distance by 3:30 or even 4 A.M.

Then there was the matter of Kirschke's light-tan knitted sport shirt, which had been taken from him when he was arrested in Victorville. Chemical analysis in the C.I.I. laboratories revealed there were tiny blood spots under the button-flap on the shirt. This had caused a flurry of excitement when the blood-type turned out to be O, the same as that of the two victims. But the excitement went glimmering when it was discovered that Kirschke's blood-type also was O. Through his attorney, Ramsey, Kirschke pointed out that he had cut himself when he broke a bottle of after-shave lotion in Las Vegas.

After listening to Lynch's recitation of the facts, O'Brien, his interest finally piqued, said, 'So we don't seem to be doing so well. It looks to me like we're running a half-assed investigation.'

'I agree,' said Lynch. 'One of the problems is that Jack Goertzen is all tied up on the Watson case and Miles Rubin is too busy running the L.A. office. If we're going to continue on this, we need a couple of full-time lawyers to supervise it.'

O'Brien said, 'We damn well *better* continue on it. If we don't we're going to take a beating politically – whitewash and all that. This case has been thrown into our lap and we just can't walk away from it. We've either got to indict and convict Kirschke, if he *is* guilty, or find the bastard who *did* commit the murders.'

'And how do you propose to do *that*?'

'Let's get the meanest, toughest son of a bitch in the office – someone from the north so they can't say he's influenced by friendship for the DA's office in L.A. – and turn him loose on this thing. Then let's team him up with someone in L.A. who's prejudiced in favor of Kirschke, going in. Like young Bob Samoian. He's such a strong law-and-order type that he's bound to think no one in law enforcement could commit this kind of murder. Let Samoian break his ass to come up with another defendant. But if he can't and our mean son of a bitch can convince him Kirschke did it, I think we'll have a case.'

'And whom do you propose as the mean son of a bitch?'

'How about Al Harris? He's the kind of guy who'd prosecute his own mother. Besides, he just lost the Dorado case before the Supreme Court, which makes him even meaner than usual.'

Lynch said, 'O.K., Harris it is.' He peered curiously at O'Brien. 'Tell me,' he said. 'What does your instinct say to you about Mr. Kirschke?'

'Right now,' replied O'Brien, 'I don't think we have a thing on him. But my instinct keeps saying to me there's something wrong with a guy who's picked up by the police and is told his wife was killed while fucking another man, and he doesn't cry or break down or get upset or show any emotion. He's cool. *Too* cool.'

Lynch nodded. He went back to his own office without mentioning Devin again.

Two days later Albert William Harris arrived in Los Angeles to take over direction of the Kirschke murder case. A medium-sized man in his late thirties with wiry, graying hair and black-rimmed glasses which gave him the appearance of a dispassionately predatory owl, he surveyed the sixth floor of the Spring Street building and selected Lynch's usually unoccupied office as his command post. He ordered an extra table and a batch of accordion files which he set, empty but anticipatory, on the table. The office soon became a replica of his own in San Francisco, except for his University of California Law School diploma and a 'Den Mother of the Year' plaque, presented to him, not without some sarcasm, by members of the San Francisco press.

His organizational activity completed, Harris went to visit his new assistant, Robert Samoian, a pudgy, round-faced, dark-haired young man who was visibly startled when his new boss walked into his office. Although Harris is Senior Assistant Attorney General in charge of the Trial and Investigations Section statewide, Samoian barely knew him because of the 400-mile geographic separation between the San Francisco and Los Angeles offices.

Harris glanced sourly at the 'Register Communists, Not Guns' sign which Samoian had tacked to his desk and asked him what staff had been lined up. Samoian said, 'We've got the best in the C.I.I. down here – Keith Byram, the agent-in-charge who's studying law, Gene Frice, a real digger who's a major in the Green Beret reserve, and Barney Allen, who's done a good job in a lot of other sticky cases. In addition, the DA has loaned us two of his top detectives full-time – Jack Gotch and Earl Cludy. We also can use St. Clair McClary and a couple of other guys from the C.I.I. if we need them.'

'Good,' said Harris. 'Have you developed a theory yet for this case?'

'All I know,' said Samoian, 'is I don't think Jack did it. He's too good a law-and-order man to get involved in something like this. The Long Beach cops think he's just great.'

'Hmmm,' said Haris. 'If that's the case, how do you think we should proceed?'

Samoian seemed prepared for the question. 'Since there were no witnesses,' he said, 'this is a circumstantial evidence case. So the way I see it, we have to look for someone who had three factors going for him – motive, means, and opportunity.'

'You're right,' Harris said. 'Did you learn that in law school?'

'No,' said Samoian, slightly abashed, 'I saw it on a Perry Mason television show.'

'Fine,' said Harris, poker-faced. 'So let's try the motive-means-opportunity test on all the other possible suspects, and if that doesn't turn up anybody, we apply motive-means-opportunity to Mr. Kirschke in the same way. O.K.?'

'O.K.,' said Samoian. He was considerably subdued.

For the next month the Harris team went through the harrowing drudgery of routine police work as they checked out all possible leads into other suspects. Harris and Samoian worked out of their command post in Lynch's office, methodically filling up the accordion files, one for each suspect and potential witness. Each morning agent-in-charge Byram would phone in and get a list of information wanted by Harris. Each evening the agents would return with reports and memos, all of which would go into the appropriate file. The accordion files began to balloon like fat garrison soldiers standing side by side on the long table.

The first possibility to be checked was that Elaine might have developed bitter enemies in the rough-and-vicious world of women's clothing manufacture. Her partner, George Jacobs, was exhaustively interviewed by Byram. Where were the clothes designed? In Los Angeles, by Elaine. Where were they manufactured? In Los Angeles. Completely in Los Angeles? No, er, as a matter of fact, we sent them across the Mexican border to be cut in Mexicali. Why? To, er, well, I guess you'd have to say, to beat the union. Was the union pissed off about this? No.

Check with the union. Genuine surprise and outrage. Don't believe they knew about the Mexican caper until we told them. Back to Jacobs. Did Elaine have any enemies here in the shop? Well, er, yes, as a matter of fact there was a cutter who said he would make fifty thousand dollars a year if she were out of the way. Check the cutter. Said he was in Mexicali all day Friday, then played poker in West Los Angeles until 2 A.M., then slept in his ex-wife's house, then flew back to Mexicali Saturday morning. Alibi all checks out with the poker players, the ex-wife, the airline ticket clerks in L.A. and Mexicali. Dead end. Motive, but no means or opportunity.

Second possibility: Mrs. Drankhan. In a love-triangle murder, the man's wife always is a possibility. Interview Mrs. Drankhan. A tall, drab, matronly woman. Separated for some time and totally resigned to the failure of the marriage. Said she spent the night of the murder at home and was visited by her mother. Interview mother. Mother confirms. Said visited friends all next day. Check with friends. No sign of Mrs. Drankhan being upset or nervous. Acted completely normally. Question Mrs. Drankhan about her knowledge of where Kirschkes lived. Convinced she had no idea. Wash this one out. Motive possible, but no means or opportunity.

Third possibility: Drankhan's other mistress. Learned about her from Mrs. Drankhan, who threw him out when she found out about their affair. A good-looking blond broad. A book-keeper at a small plant near Drankhan's shop. Had been shacking up with him three nights a week when he not busy with Elaine. Interview her. Said she was supposed to help Drankhan with his books in his office on Saturday morning. Spent Friday night at home. On Saturday morning a girl friend from Alhambra came by and asked her to help decorate her apartment. Told the friend she couldn't because Bill was coming by. At noon she gave up waiting and went to friend in Alhambra. Stayed until Monday morning. Kept phoning her apartment to see if Drankhan had arrived. Another girl friend with her in Alhambra, too, on Sunday and Monday.

Check the girl friends. They confirm she was completely normal on Saturday and Sunday aside from being upset over not hearing from Drankhan. No evidence of post-homicide anxiety. On other hand, she broke down completely when she heard on the radio that Drankhan had been killed. She couldn't be that good an actress to hold up through Saturday and Sunday. Also, am convinced through interrogation that she didn't even know about Elaine, though suspected Drankhan did have someone else. Scratch this one on lack of means and opportunity, as well as another important factor in circumstantial evidence cases – consciousness of guilt.

The fourth possibility took the most time. It was the one that Kirschke and his attorney, Ramsey, kept repeating in their barrage of interviews and press conferences about the case. On the KNXT interview program *Viewpoint*, for example, Kirschke said, 'It was some dope-crazed burglar who surprised Elaine and Bill and shot his way out – probably a criminal I once convicted who wanted revenge.' Ramsey kept insisting that the revenge-bent criminal had fired the fatal shots through the window from which the screen had been removed.

C.I.I. agents Byram, Frice, and Allen had to go through every one of the hundreds of cases handled in the courts by Kirschke throughout his years as an Assistant DA. Then, after exhaustive interrogation of District Attorney and court personnel, they did find one man who, when sent to prison by Kirschke, said, 'I'll get you.' They scoured the state for the man, now released from prison. They finally found him in Northern California, where he had started a new life under a new name. But he had never left town the weekend of the murder. A half-dozen witnesses attested to that fact.

When all the other possibilities were eliminated, Harris said to Samoian, 'All right now, let's concentrate on our friend Kirschke.' Samoian nodded glumly. Harris reached for one of the accordion files. It was labeled 'Kirschke, J.,' and it had been fattening more than the others because even while the agents were looking into the alternative suspects, they were gathering information on Kirschke, too. 'O.K.,' said Harris. 'Let's divide this stuff under the same criteria – motive, means, and opportunity.'

As Harris opened the file to review the evidence, O'Brien was in the hospital, making his fifth visit of the week to the bedside of his son, Devin. The boy's pelvic bones had knit satisfactorily and most of the pain was gone. But O'Brien noted that Devin was getting fat. 'My God,' he said to Marie, 'is he *really* going to be a eunuch?'

CHAPTER SIX

It was 8:05 P.M. that night and twilight already had settled on the little oil-refinery, lemon-growing town of Santa Paula, nestled in a valley about thirty-three miles east of Santa Barbara, California. A dim lamp shone through the windows of the shabby shacklike house at 135 South 4th Street as two men came walking down the street toward it. The men were hippie types, in T-shirts and bell-bottoms, and with long hair and flowing moustaches.

The two men, in their early twenties, approached the door of the house and knocked. After an interval a voice from inside asked, 'Yeah, who is it?'

One of the men said, 'It's Jim, come to see Unk. He's expecting me.'

The door opened cautiously, and then wider to admit them. Inside, two young girls and about six youths were sprawled about on a beat-up couch and bed. A Rolling Stones record was playing and there was the faint acrid smell of stale marijuana smoke lingering in the room. The occupants of the room obviously were on much stronger stuff. There were fresh needle marks in their arms.

'Where's Unk?' Jim asked the man who had admitted them. The doorkeeper inclined his head toward the kitchen. Jim and his companion went into the other room of the two-room house. A hulking, huge-muscled man stood there, his arm bared, a hypodermic needle in his hand. The man, about twenty-six, stared suspiciously at Jim's friend. 'Oh,' said Jim, 'this here is Frank, the guy I told you about when I bought the shit from you the other day.' Unk nodded and turned his attention back to the hypodermic. 'Do you mind?' he said. 'There's been so many people knocking at the door I can't even get a good fix.'

Unk finished injecting himself with heroin and said, 'All right, let's get down to business. What about the guns?'

Frank said, 'Well, we're going to pull a job down in L.A. at a sporting goods store and we want to trade guns for some smack.'

Unk said, 'Yeah, I see what you mean, but I'll have to talk to my connection.'

'Is that Squeak?' Jim asked.

'Yeah,' said Unk. 'What kind of guns can you get?'

Frank spoke for the first time. He said, 'We can get chromed or blued automatics, anything you want.'

Unk's eyes lit up. He suddenly left them and went into the other room. When he came back, he had a wicked-looking 9 mm pistol in his hand. He said, 'Here, take a look at this.'

Frank said, 'Say, those guns are hard to get. It's a Luger, isn't it?'

Unk said, 'Yeah, it's in good shape and it's never been registered anywhere.'

Frank said dryly, 'We can do better. But right now we came to buy some shit. How much stuff you got?'

A regretful look came over Unk's face. 'All I got left is two grams. Do you want that?'

'O.K., but I really wanted a quarter ounce. How much for the two grams?'

'Seventy dollars, but Squeak'll be here later and I can get you a good price on a quarter. Can you come back?'

'Yeah,' said Frank. 'What time?'

'About eleven. And if you have some guns in your pad, why don't you bring them to show Squeak. Maybe we can set up a deal for after you pull the job on the sporting goods store.'

'We got three pieces,' said Jim, 'but they're not for sale now.'

'Yeah, I know,' said Unk, 'but Squeak would just like to see what you can produce in the way of pieces.'

Unk went out and came back with two plastic bags of white powder. Frank then gave Unk four twenty-dollar bills and got a ten-dollar bill back in change. He and Jim then left. As they walked through the living room, someone was copulating with a young girl on the couch.

At 11:30 P.M. Jim and Frank returned to the house on South 4th Street. They went through the now even more crowded living room and into the kitchen. Unk was there – alone. He pointed to the attaché case Jim was carrying and asked, 'Do you have the guns?' Jim opened the case and handed Unk three .38's. Unk examined them with undisguised admiration, and at that moment a huge form loomed up in the doorway to the living room. It was a young man in his twenties, six feet four inches tall, blond, blue-eyed, magnificently proportioned, and handsome enough to be a movie star. He wore red-and-white-striped slacks and a powder-blue knit shirt that was carefully designed to emphasize his muscles.

The newcomer said, 'Is your name Jim?'

Jim said, 'It is. And I guess you're Squeak?'

'Right,' said Squeak, and he took the three guns from Unk and carefully examined them.

Then Squeak turned back to Jim and said, 'How much dust you want for fifty guns?'

Jim said, 'Five ounces.'

Squeak said, 'O.K., but in the shipment I want .45's, .38's, and 9 millimeter automatics. And I also want the shipment to include three machine guns and two grease guns.'

'You got a deal,' said Jim.

'O.K.,' said Squeak, 'how much stuff you want now – a quarter?'

'Yeah,' said Frank.

Squeak reached into his shirt pocket and pulled out a red balloon. He shook the balloon, and ten capsules, each filled with white heroin powder, spilled out. He said, 'This is bitching heroin. Look around at all the people who are fucked up on this stuff.' He pointed to the sprawl of bodies in the living room.

He then wrapped the capsules in a cleansing tissue and handed them to Jim. Jim gave him a hundred and twenty dollars.

Jim said, 'Tell me, did you ever have to swallow a balloon?'

'Yeah,' chuckled Squeak. 'The pigs picked me up one time and I swallowed a balloon with fifteen caps in it. I was constipated and I didn't shit it out for two days, and by that time I was out on bail. They just got me for pot.'

He shook hands with Jim and Frank and said, 'When you're ready to deal for the guns, just call Unk. You got his number. I don't have a phone at my pad.'

Jim and Frank left. They walked down the street, around

the corner and into an alley. A black Ford sedan was waiting for them there. They got in and the car sped away. Driving the Ford was Sixto Ramirez. Next to him was Roger Livingston. Both are agents of the Attorney General's Bureau of Narcotic Control. Jim was Detective Russ Moeller and Frank was Detective Walter Frazier of the Ventura County Sheriff's Department. The operation was planned and executed by Livingston.

Moeller and Frazier gave Livingston a verbal report on everything that had happened that night. Livingston then transmitted the information, via the car's private-channel radio, to his BNE field supervisor, George Houston, who passed it on to agent-in-charge Gerard Shoemaker – and the report eventually ended up on O'Brien's desk.

CHAPTER SEVEN

At the time Albert Harris began his review of the possible case against Jack Kirschke, several significant developments had taken place regarding the life, times, and peregrinations of the Assistant District Attorney. Much of this discovery was the work of C.I.I. agent Gene Frice, a wiry blondish man who had had more experience with murder cases than anyone else in the department. Also Frice had one of the more interesting backgrounds.

In his late forties and with the mien of a college-professor grandfather (he *does* have one grandchild in addition to his five children), he had served as a paratrooper in the 82nd Airborne Division in World War II, jumped into Normandy, learned radio and demolition guerrilla techniques, was called back in the Korean War as an Army Criminal Investigation specialist, and later ended up as a Green Beret major and executive officer of a Special Forces Company. In between, he got a bachelor's and a master's degree from Cal State and was studying for a Ph.D. in Government and Public Service at the University of Southern California.

In the meantime he also got married (his wife, Margaret, still is a registered nurse at a San Fernando Valley hospital), and he worked for eight years as an investigator in the Public Defender's Office in Los Angeles. It was here, and also in the Army CID, that he investigated more than thirty murder cases – in addition to the rape charges which, despite his efforts as a defense expert, resulted in Caryl Chessman's dying in the gas chamber.

In 1961, looking for more stimulating and better-paying work, Frice took the civil service examination for C.I.I. agent in the Attorney General's Department of Justice. His record had been brilliant since then, interrupted only by call-ups of his Green Beret Reserve outfit. That's what worried him now. If the Kirschke case was not solved by summer, he might find himself practicing insurgency somewhere thousands of miles away.

It was the tidy-minded Ph.D. candidate Frice who had

been most appalled at the way the Long Beach Police Department had botched up the Kirschke murder scene. He wrote in a report:

> There were no diagrams, no measurements, no color photos. The distances from the round bed in a square room were not worked out for us. We had to spend days figuring out where those people were lying on that bed. The Long Beach police violated all procedure by stomping around the room instead of photographing it from the door-sill.

Almost immediately Frice had conflicts with the Long Beach detective assigned to work with him on the case, Garold E. McIntyre, who previously had been a petty theft investigator. McIntyre knew Kirschke and his wife, admired Kirschke as an excellent DA, and expected him to be appointed to a judgeship. McIntyre's first theory was that the Elaine Kirschke–Drankhan deaths were a clear classic case of murder-suicide. He was astounded when he rolled Drankhan's body over and there was no gun there.

A week or more after the investigation started, McIntyre approached Frice, who by now was working with another Long Beach detective named Robert Castillo, with whom he found himself more compatible. McIntyre pulled a piece of paper out of his pocket and showed it to Frice. McIntyre said, 'I've been carrying this around for some time now. I found it in Jack's dresser drawer. Do you think it's important?'

Frice glanced at the paper, turned white, and said, 'You're goddam right it's important.' The paper was a note in Elaine's handwriting. It obviously was an agreement she had drawn up to govern her relations with her husband some time before. The note stated:

> We will live together until May 1, 1967, in separate bedrooms, but without sexual provocation or invitation.
>
> Thereafter, for a one-year trial period, we will cohabit with the understanding that neither one will seek out the companionship of the opposite sex in any manner.
>
> Until May 1, 1967, each one agrees to inform the other

of all unplanned activities whatsoever in whatever social activities either party should be involved in.

Frice rushed back to the office and showed the paper to Harris. Before he popped it into the accordion file, a rare hint of animation crossed Harris's face. 'Can we use it?' Frice asked. 'I doubt it,' said Harris. 'The judge probably will throw it out as evidence because of the way it was taken without a warrant. But this is the first time I figure we might be on the right track.'

'How so?' asked Samoian.

'Because we have caught Mr. Kirschke in a lie,' said Harris. 'Remember how he told Goertzen and Rubin he was living a normal happy married life with Elaine?' He held up the paper. 'What's normal and happy about *this?*'

All during the time Frice and the other investigators were checking out suspects other than Kirschke, bits and pieces of information about the murders had kept coming in, to bloat the accordion files on Harris's table. The lab technicians, for example, were able to reconstruct the scene at the exact instant the fatal bullets were fired.

When the bodies had been found, Elaine was lying on her back in the round bed; Drankhan no longer was beside her; he was face down on the floor alongside the bed, his nose submerged in a pool of his own vomit. Microscopic sperm analysis told the technicians that the couple had completed sexual intercourse just prior to their demise. By painstakingly examining huge photographic blowups of the bedspread on which Elaine and Drankhan had been lying, defined indentations – a hand mark here, a buttock mark there, etc. – told them that the couple had been lying on their backs in post-coital repose, Elaine's head on Drankhan's shoulder, when they abruptly expired.

The puzzle of why Drankhan was face down on the *floor* was solved when the medical autopsy reports came in. The key to the puzzle was a phenomenon called lividity. When a human being dies, all the blood in the body soon settles, by gravity, to the lowest parts of the corpse, according to its position. In Drankhan's case, even though he was lying face down on the floor, all the blood was in his *back*, and had congealed there. Since blood in a corpse cannot flow upward, the technicians deduced that Drankhan had died in bed, on his back, as the indentations in the bedspread had indicated. He was very close to the edge of the bed. So, as lividity set in, with the weight of his blood concentrating in his back, there was enough of a shift in his center of gravity to cause him to roll off the bed, thus ending up in his face-down position on the floor. The vomit then would spew forth naturally, even though Drankhan had been dead for some time.

Frice saw this report late one afternoon. He stared at it thoughtfully, had it Xeroxed, and took a copy home with him. He studied the report again at home and then startled his wife, Margaret, by going into the bedroom and deliberately rolling off the edge of their bed several times. Each time his knee or some other bony part of his body hit the floor, there was a sharp report.

After dinner Frice soaked his bruised knees in his bathtub, got dressed, and drove the more than forty miles from his home in Tujunga, in the San Fernando Valley, to the Kirschke apartment in Naples, on the coast. He let himself into the apartment, and for a long time he studied the place where the round bed had stood (it had been removed for evidence). Finally, seemingly satisfied, he turned to go. Then idly he looked up at the ceiling lighting fixture in the bedroom. He got a chair, climbed up on it, and unscrewed the light bulb from the fixture. He shook the bulb and noted that it was burned out.

The ballistics reports had come in from the lab a day or two later. One bullet apparently had creased Drankhan's forehead, killed Elaine by ripping through her skull, and then imbedded itself in the lavender quilted headboard. The second bullet, the one that killed Drankhan, had fragmented. Working mostly with the headboard bullet, the technicians determined that the shots were fired by an extremely rare weapon, a .38 caliber Harrington and Richards Defender, a few thousand of which had been bought by the U.S. Government many years ago for use by the Federal Postal Inspectors. One of the ballistics men noted that he had seen only two such guns in his nineteen years of working with weapons. The technician wrote in his report:

This bullet also might possibly have been fired by a Spanish gun, but I doubt it. The Harrington and Richards makes striations on a bullet that are distinctive. It has six grooves in the barrel, instead of the standard five.

Agent-in-charge Keith Byram immediately put his men to work tracking down the records of any H and R Defenders that had turned up in previous crimes in California. They scoured police files throughout the state, and finally Barney Allen came up with an interesting find. An H and R Defender, serial number 22068, had been the weapon in the kidnap-robbery of a market owner by one James Vernon Mitchell in October, 1961. The crime had been committed in Long Beach. The Assistant DA who had prosecuted and convicted Mitchell was Jack Kirschke.

Without waiting for instructions, Allen went to the District Attorney's office and checked the records of the Mitchell case. He finally came upon what he was looking for. There was a receipt for a .38 caliber Harrington and Richards Defender, serial number 22068, with four shells, taken out of evidence as a souvenir with the permission of the judge after Mitchell had been convicted. The receipt was dated January 3, 1962. The man who took the gun as a souvenir and who signed the receipt was Jack Kirschke.

Byram, Frice, and Allen were too experienced as investigators to get carried away by this discovery. They knew it only meant that Kirschke once had owned a gun *similar* to the murder weapon. Unless the Kirschke gun, serial number 22068, could be found and test-fired to determine if its ballistics matched up with the death bullets, the mere fact of his possessing it would amount to nothing in court. But number 22068 could *not* be found. Kirschke had told the police he used to keep it in the drawer of his bedside table, but it had disappeared from there. Byram had had the entire area searched and even had the canals dragged under the bridges leading to Naples, but there was no sign of Number 22068.

Nonetheless, Frice doggedly set out to trace the history of this particular gun. Through phone calls to the Post Office Department in Washington, he learned that the Postal Inspectors had been armed with the H and R's for eight years and then all of them had been replaced and sold to a Washington, D.C., wholesaler. The wholesaler had marketed them to dealers throughout the country. Number 22068 had been sold in 1956 to David M. Weinstein, owner of the United Sporting Goods store in Long Beach. Weinstein told Frice he had the gun in his store for three years. He then sold it to a customer who returned it. It next was stolen from Weinstein in a robbery of his store but was given back to him by the police when the thief was apprehended. Number 22068 thereupon was sold again by Weinstein in February, 1961, to Jack F. Norton. It was not known how the gun got into the hands of kidnapper-robber James Vernon Mitchell.

There was something about this history that vaguely disturbed Frice. But at the moment he couldn't put his finger on what it was.

Actually, Frice had something more immediate that troubled him, and he spent a lot of his spare time in the Kirschke apartment trying to figure it out. This was the question of where the shots had been fired from. Frice kept studying the bedroom where Elaine Kirschke and Drankhan had been killed, and several times he summoned a C.I.I. photographer to photograph it from still another angle. He also made a rough sketch of the bedroom (shown overleaf), which he carried with him and puzzled over constantly.

The first possibility was that the shots had come from outside, through the ground-floor bedroom window, as Kirschke kept insisting (usually, as he said in his many interviews, 'by some revenge-maddened criminal, who removed the window screen'). Frice quickly eliminated this theory from his mind. He already knew, from the lab reports of the trajectory of the bullets and the location of the major bloodstains, that the shots had come from the opposite side of the room, directly *across* from the window. He interviewed all the policemen who had been on the scene after the bodies had been discovered, and finally he found an inexperienced motorcycle officer who sheepishly admitted that *he* had taken the screen off the window and left it lying on the ground.

This left the possibility of the closet. From the very beginning it had been the theory of Inspector Garold McIntyre

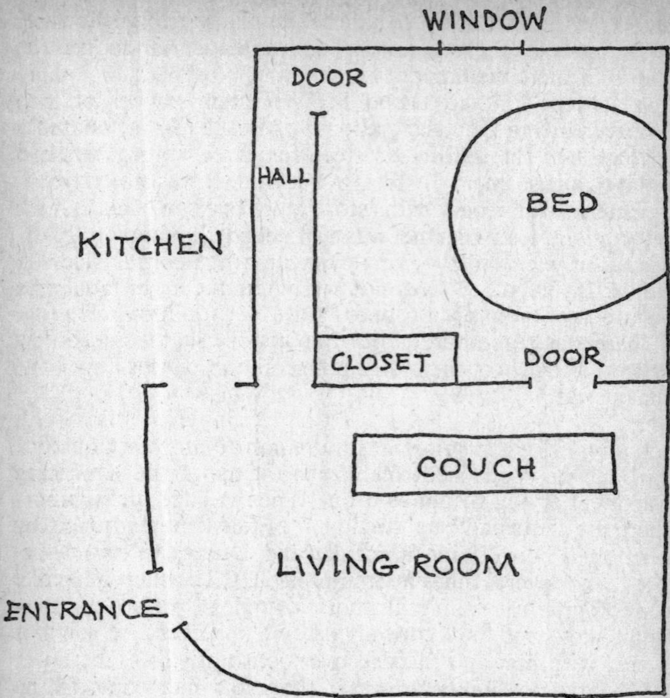

of the Long Beach Police, often stated in interviews, that the killer had hidden in the closet and shot the victims after throwing open the closet door when they had finished intercourse. But Frice could not buy this theory, either. The shots *could* have been fired from the closet, but such a line-of-fire just did not quite match up with the trajectory plotted by the crime lab.

Where else? One afternoon Frice was studying his sketch and his eye fell on the marks he had made for the unused door between the bedroom and the living room. He had thought of this door before, but it had seemed unlikely, with all the junk piled up against it behind the couch.

That evening Frice went to the apartment again. He slid in behind the couch, and he found a gap in the welter of stored books and paintings there, just large enough for him to set his feet on top of a rolled-up carpet which clogged the space against the door.

Frice flung the door open. It opened easily to his left into the bedroom side of the wall. With the door ajar, he had a perfect view of the entire area where the round bed had once been.

These were the reports, along with many others, which Albert Harris discussed with his task force when he finally got around to reviewing any possible case against Kirschke. As he had promised Samoian, he broke the facts down into the three categories of motive, means, and opportunity. When he was finished, Harris had doodled the following outline:

MOTIVE: (1) Jealousy over wife having affair with Drankhan. But did he know about it?
(2) If he did, fear about scandal surfacing and ruining his chances for judgeship.
(3) The marital agreement handwritten by Elaine. Indicates stormy previous relationship. Contrary to what Kirschke told us.

MEANS: (1) Kirschke the only suspect to own a Harrington and Richards Defender.
(2) But it could only be coincidence that he had same model as the murder weapon. He took other guns out of evidence as souvenirs, too.
(3) Also no indication that Kirschke ever previously even fired the gun or knew how to fire it. The killer was quite a marksman – two shots, two corpses.

OPPORTUNITY: (1) Kirschke the only suspect who knew how to find his way through the twisting streets and alleys of Rivo Alto Canal. Even our men got lost there.
(2) Kirschke the only suspect who possibly could know best place to fire shots was from unused door behind couch in living room. A stranger to the apartment would

have gone down hall to regular door of the bedroom.

(3) All this means nothing and Kirschke is in the clear if, as he said, he left airport at 11 P.M., arrived at Yermo gas station at 3:30 A.M., and at Las Vegas at dawn.

When he finished the outline, Harris stared at it. 'It's a weak case,' he said.

'Does that mean we're going to give up?' asked Samoian.

'No,' said Harris. 'We're all going to go out in the field and we're going to see what else we can dig up in the areas of motive, means, and opportunity.'

So the entire task force went out into the field to interview every possible neighbor, friend, and associate of Kirschke's. Even the two lawyers, Harris and Samoian, were out pushing doorbells. At one point Harris teamed up with Byram, and Samoian with Allen, and the two teams covered both sides of Rivo Alto Canal, talking with the occupants of all houses and apartments in the neighborhood. Once, after listening to Harris cross-examine a ten-year-old, Byram – who was about to become a lawyer – burst out laughing. When Harris glowered at him, Byram said, 'It's just that a few months ago you were arguing one of the most important cases in history before the Supreme Court, and here you are pounding a beat like a cop.'

In their concerted effort the task force did come up with some helpful information. They uncovered nothing to bolster the 'opportunity' phase of the case, but there was an interesting addendum to the 'means' argument. One neighbor said that Kirschke previously *had* used the Harrington and Richards Defender, and knew how to use it well. The neighbor explained that he and his wife had taken a cruise down the Baja California coast with Kirschke in his sloop and Kirschke had spent most of his time firing the H and R, with good accuracy, at targets along the deserted Mexican coastline.

But most of the new information came in the area of 'motive'. The task force began to build up a picture of bitter intramarital strife between Kirschke and Elaine that was in further direct variance with Kirschke's cool assertions of domestic tranquillity with his wife, and that he had no knowledge – and therefore no bitterness – about her affair with Drankhan.

First, the upstairs neighbor, Frank Cornell, said that he frequently had heard 'shouting and a racket' in the Kirschke apartment below, but that he didn't really know what was going on. Once, however, he heard Elaine scream, 'Stop it, stop it! You're hurting me!' Then, 'All right, stop it, stop it, stop it! I'll tell you.'

Next, Cornell's son-in-law, twenty-two-year-old James Miller, a reserve Deputy Sheriff, told the investigators that he had heard a similar altercation while he was visiting the Cornells on Christmas Day. He had peered in a window of the Kirschke apartment and had seen Kirschke pinning Elaine up against the wall of the dining room and 'beating the shit out of her.'

Then came a tearful statement from Sharon Lyle, Kirschke's pretty secretary, whom he had unsuccessfully attempted to seduce. Miss Lyle told the investigators Kirschke had said to her one day that he had beaten Elaine until he got the name of her boy friend out of her. The name was Bill.

Finally, purely by accident, the task force stumbled on some of the most interesting information of all. One day Keith Byram and Jack Gotch, one of the DA's investigators, were out ringing doorbells in the neighborhood when they came upon Mrs. Patricia Katz, a middle-aged blond divorcée. The investigators subsequently learned that Pat Katz was a member of a group of ladies in their forties and fifties who were unofficially known as 'The Jolly Girls' in the swinging yacht club society of Naples and that Elaine Kirschke had been known as one of the foremost members of the group.

When Byram and Gotch first met Mrs. Katz, she told them that one night just a week before the murders Kirschke had severely beaten Elaine and that Elaine had come running over to her house and was cowering in the bushes. She was afraid to come inside because, Elaine had told her, 'Jack knows every closet in your house and will find me.'

Byram then went to see another Jolly Girl, Norma McIntire, who, Pat Katz said also had witnessed the cowering-in-the-bushes incident. 'Yes, that's exactly what happened,' said Mrs. McIntire. 'Elaine was frightened, upset, and terribly bruised. I put her in my car and took her home with me. She told me she had said to Jack, "Why don't you get a gun and shoot me?" '

From Norma McIntire, the trail naturally led to a third Jolly Girl, Marma Herfter. 'I often saw black-and-blue marks on Elaine's arms,' Mrs. Herfter told Byram, 'and once she had some badly bruised ribs. I asked her about them at a party and she said, "They're much better. I'm just lucky Jack didn't break my neck." '

When Al Harris read the Jolly Girl reports, he picked up the phone and placed a call to Kirschke's attorney, the Silver Fox. Harris said to Ramsey, 'Your client's statements were unsatisfactory when he met with our people in your office. I'd like to talk with Mr. Kirschke, and maybe he can clarify some points. A discussion with us might help him.'

Ramsey said, formally, 'My client absolutely declines to discuss the matter.'

'Are you sure?' asked Harris.

'Positive,' said Ramsey.

After he had exchanged cool good-byes with Ramsey, Harris sat thinking for a few minutes. Then he said to Samoian, 'Tom Lynch and Charlie O'Brien are in town. I think we'd better go in and see them. I have an idea.'

Actually, Lynch was in Sacramento, so the meeting was held there. Harris took Samoian, Byram, and Frice with him, and all four detailed the case to Lynch and O'Brien. The recitation lasted for two hours. When it was over, O'Brien said, 'It's not a strong case. The gas station alibi louses you up.'

Harris said, 'Yes, I know. That's why I want to try something I think never has been done before. I want to go to the Grand Jury and instead of just putting on the usual skeleton case to get an indictment, I'd like to call *all* the witnesses, including the gas station boys. In other words, I want to get an appraisal from the *jury* as to whether we have a chance to win this thing or not. If the Grand Jury believes Kirschke's strongest witnesses, they won't indict. If they don't believe them, or have doubts, they *will* indict. I'm willing to take a chance and let *them* decide.'

'An interesting idea,' said O'Brien. 'Sort of like a movie company letting the critics read a script in advance before they decide whether or not to make the movie.' He looked over at Lynch. 'It's my opinion that we should go with it.'

'Go,' said Lynch.

On their way out, Frice lagged behind and walked down the corridor with O'Brien. He said to the Chief Deputy, 'I heard about your boy. I'm sorry.'

O'Brien, annoyed that the news of Devin's accident had gotten around to this extent, grunted his appreciation.

'I just want to tell you one thing,' said Frice. 'I have a boy, my youngest, Mark. When Mark was a year old, he fell in a lake and drowned. He had no heartbeat or pulse. There was a doctor there and he said there was no hope, but my wife, Margaret, kept doing mouth-to-mouth resuscitation, and after thirty-six minutes Mark started to breathe again.'

O'Brien was listening intently now. Frice continued: 'When they got Mark to the hospital, they found out that since his heart had stopped beating for so long, there was no oxygen going to the brain and he had suffered bad brain damage. They told us that if the boy lived, he'd probably be mentally defective. He was, too. For more than a year Mark was spastic and couldn't speak at all. I just want you to know that Mark is six now, and he's just as bright and as sharp and as normal as my other four kids. They're pretty resilient, you know.'

O'Brien exhaled noticeably and put his arm on Frice's shoulder, a rare emotional gesture for him. 'Thanks, Gene,' he said.

CHAPTER EIGHT

The next seven days were a week of news and decisions for O'Brien.

On Saturday morning he and Marie went to the hospital, and they found Devin sitting up in a wheelchair. The doctors expected that he might be walking soon.

On Monday O'Brien had to stay in Northern California to make two political speeches, one of the requirements of his job. For the first time since the accident to Devin, the Chief Deputy was more like his usually salty self. In San Francisco, after he discussed air pollution and the Santa Barbara Channel oil spill, he was heckled by a supporter of Los Angeles District Attorney Evelle Younger, who was planning to run as a Republican candidate for Attorney General. The heckler stated, 'Mr. Younger says that the Attorney General's office has been weak on the environmental issue, that it has a lot of unused muscle.'

'The only unused muscle I know,' retorted O'Brien, 'is between Mr. Younger's ears.'

At lunch in Fresno that day, O'Brien spoke to a group of law enforcement officers. When he finished, George T. Davis, another potential candidate for the Attorney Generalship, rose and said, 'Say, what about the El Paso Natural Gas scandal?'

'What about the Johnstown flood?' snapped O'Brien, walking off the stage.

On his way out, the Chief Deputy was cornered by the editor of an underground newspaper. 'Where do you stand on giving the vote to the eighteen-year-olds?' the editor demanded. 'I'm *for* it,' replied O'Brien. Having expected an argument, the editor, a youth of about twenty, continued to belabor the point. 'Look,' cut in O'Brien, 'I already told you. I'm *for* it.'

'Well,' persisted the editor, 'how *long* have you been for it?'

'Since I was eighteen,' said O'Brien, and he popped into his car and headed back to his office.

Tom McDonald had accompanied O'Brien on the political tour, and they chatted intermittently on the long ride from Fresno to San Francisco. O'Brien told McDonald about his conversation with Gene Frice and about the agony the agent had suffered over his nearly drowned child. 'How little we know about the personal lives of the people we work with,' he said. 'We're supposed to be cold-blooded mechanical prosecutors. No one thinks of us as having personal lives and personal pain and problems and hangups like everyone else. There's young Ron George, one of the best attorneys we've got, working his ass off for a lousy – for him – twenty-two hundred dollars a month, when he and his father own thousands of acres in the San Joaquin Valley. Sure, he *might* get a judgeship or get started in politics because he worked for us, but then again he might not. Why does he do it? Then there's Leroy Sana, maybe our best agent in the L.A. office, with his wife in a wheelchair. Someone told me the other day she has one of those rare muscle diseases . . . '.

O'Brien stopped talking abruptly and sat in silence for a few minutes. Then he picked up the microphone of the car's two-way radio and asked for O. J. Hawkins, the assistant director of his Department of Justice. 'From now on,' he told Hawkins, 'only give Los Angeles assignments to Leroy Sana. I want him to be able to get home every night.'

When he arrived at his San Francisco office, O'Brien had time for only one appointment before flying to Los Angeles. He saw Eric Collins, whose cases included the Father Nikliborc matter and the wave of art frauds. O'Brien looked up at the towering Collins and said, 'Just tell me about the good father. I'll get a report on art frauds from Andrea Ordin later this week in Los Angeles.' 'The good father,' said Collins with a frown, 'keeps looking less good all the time.'

'What have you found out?' asked O'Brien.

'We've got his background,' said Collins. 'He comes from Chicago and graduated in 1951 from St. Mary's of the Lake Seminary in Mundelein, Illinois. Then he came out here to the West Coast, went to the Immaculate Heart Seminary in San Diego, and was ordained a priest in 1955.'

'Really a priest?'

'Yes, I'm afraid so. He was ordained by old Bishop

Charles Buddy down there, but I'm sure the old boy didn't know what was going to happen. In 1957 he appointed Father Nikliborc to be an assistant to Father Nightengale, who ran Boys Town of the Desert for the diocese. Father Nikliborc was put in charge of handling all the money from the mail solicitations for the home, which is operated by the Brothers of Charity of the Immaculate Heart of Mary, a specially created order of the San Diego diocese. For your information, the home is for orphan boys up to seventeen years old. It was founded as an Indian school by the Franciscan monks about seventy-five years ago, and it looks it. The place is in dreadful shape.'

'You say Father Robert was put in charge of the till?'

'Yes, and he's continued to handle all money matters as president and financial director, long after Father Nightengale was transferred out.'

'Where does the money come from?'

'Well, at first it all came in from mail solicitations. Then Father Robert got involved with a character he knew back in Chicago, a man who calls himself Colonel Harold McClintock, and he made deals with big companies to give Boys Town items of salvage – such as obsolete machinery or business forms – which Father Robert and McClintock then sold to salvage dealers.'

'McClintock,' said O'Brien, wrinkling his forehead. 'Is that the bird who got into trouble soliciting money back East for the Disabled American Veterans?'

'One and the same,' said Collins. 'Only he isn't a colonel and his name isn't McClintock. It's Harold Sager. We found that out by writing to the Attorney General of Illinois. The AG there notified us that he had gotten a court injunction ordering Sager to cease and desist and refrain from soliciting funds on behalf of the Disabled American Veterans or any other charitable organization.'

'So Mr. Sager just transferred his activities out here?'

'I'm afraid so. He had a deal with Father Robert to keep forty-nine per cent of the net and he must have made a bloody fortune.' Collins pulled out a list. 'Here are some of the items they got big corporations to donate. Fifty thousand surgical needles, a hundred and ninety thousand loose-leaf binders, furniture, trucks, tractors, IBM cards, generators, drill presses. The corporations took a big charitable deduction on their tax returns, and Father Robert and the Colonel took in a big chunk of profit when they sold the stuff.'

'Pretty clever. But how much of the money went to Boys Town of the Desert?'

'Ay, there's the rub,' said Collins. 'There are indications that as much as forty thousand dollars a week was coming in, but Boys Town never reported income of more than fifty thousand dollars a *year*. Some years their reported income was as low as six or seven thousand dollars.'

O'Brien whistled. He said, 'I presume you've had a little chat with the good father by now.'

'Yes,' said Collins, 'I called him in to the office here, and he couldn't be more charming. He's a nice-looking young chap of about thirty-seven. When I discussed the Colonel with him, he said, "I'll do business with the devil himself if it brings in money for Boys Town." But he agreed to sever his relationship with Sager. Then I asked him how he was able to bank a half million dollars in his own name when he had no provable source of income. The good father had an answer for that, too. He said the money was given to him by an unnamed donor whose name he pledged by confessional seal not to divulge. Needless to say, I checked with the diocese in San Diego. They were very uncooperative at first, saying that Boys Town of the Desert is a private corporation and not directly under their financial jurisdiction, but finally I got Bishop Furey – who replaced Bishop Buddy – to give me an affidavit saying that such an anonymous donation as described by Father Nikliborc is *not* a proper use of the confessional seal.'

By now O'Brien was taking notes. He asked, 'When Father Nikliborc was in your office, did you ask him about his double life as Robert Drew Rand, the Las Vegas and Palm Springs swinger?'

'Yes,' said Collins, 'and he explained it all by saying he needed such a double identity to be effective as a fund raiser. I didn't pursue the point further because I didn't want him to know we knew about his bowling team, his girls and gambling in Las Vegas, his horses, his Cadillacs, or *this*.' Collins pulled a paper out of his pocket and showed it to

O'Brien. It was a quitclaim deed, filed February 10, 1960, in the Riverside County Courthouse. The deed read:

> Nancy J. Rand, a married woman, hereby remise, release and forever quitclaim to Robert D. Rand, her husband, the following described property
>
> Lot 13 Vista La Palmas
>
> (signed) Nancy J. Rand

'Lot 13, Vista La Palmas,' explained Collins, 'is the house at 1194 Vista Vispero Drive in Palm Springs, which is owned by Father Nikliborc. It's the property he bought from Tony Martin and Cyd Charisse.'

O'Brien said, 'I think this case has progressed beyond what can be handled by a charitable trust investigator like John Fiscus. Ask the C.I.I. to put a good *criminal* agent on it.'

O'Brien flew to Los Angeles late that afternoon, spent his usual restless night amid the less-than-soundproof walls of the Lo-tel Motel, and arrived at his office early Tuesday morning.

Executive assistant Tom McDonald, playing with the flowing moustache of his Mephistophelian red beard, looked at the Chief Deputy uncertainly from behind the piles of newspapers which habitually barricade his desk. McDonald hadn't seen much of O'Brien since the accident to Devin, and when he did, O'Brien was quiet and subdued and far from his old curmudgeon self. This time O'Brien opened the conversation with one of his better aphorisms. He grunted, 'There are nuts who run the world and nuts who move through it,' and McDonald automatically knew that O'Brien was getting back to normal.

McDonald followed O'Brien into his office, carrying a sheaf of papers in his hand. The executive assistant, a former reporter in the Los Angeles bureau of the *New York Times*, threw an attention-grabbing headline at his boss. 'Sheila's pregnant,' he said. O'Brien stared at him in utter amazement since he knew that McDonald and his stunningly beautiful wife, Sheila, long ago had despaired of the possibility of having a baby naturally and had adopted two infants. O'Brien stifled any temptation to wax sentimental and grumbled, 'It's about time. Took you eleven years, didn't it?' McDonald smiled his boyish smile. O'Brien *was* getting back to normal.

They went to work on the new cases that had come into the office, with McDonald ushering the attorneys and agents in and out of O'Brien's office, to explain and amplify. The cases were the usual weekly bag, ten or twelve of them. O'Brien knew that some of the cases would come to nothing, that others would be settled with out-of-court consent decrees and fines, that others were four or five years away from final judgment in the appeals courts. Maybe only one case out of the twelve would even *reach* the courts. But each, for a half-hour or so, required all the attention and concentration he devoted to, say, the Kirschke murder case. Otherwise, O'Brien knew, he was not doing his job.

There was a complaint against a group of Palm Springs judges who were accused of accepting loans from lawyer friends after bestowing on them lucrative trusteeships to handle the financial affairs of the wealthy Agua Caliente tribe of Indians. There was a pending multimillion-dollar suit against General Motors, Ford, and Chrysler for conspiring to prevent the installation of antismog devices, as prescribed by California law. Another case against General Motors was for unrealistic suggested retail list prices on the window stickers of its new cars.

There were briefs on behalf of the People of California in the Supreme Court to protect access to public beaches through private property. There was a case against a fire extinguisher company whose door-to-door salesmen posed as Los Angeles Fire Department inspectors checking on faulty fire extinguishers that had to be replaced. There was a disciplinary action against four of O'Brien's own Bureau of Narcotic Enforcement agents who were drinking before they participated in a narcotics raid, in which a policeman from another agency accidentally shot an innocent bystander. There were developing indications of a gigantic land swindle, including the bribery of Los Angeles city officials, in a planned golf course-estate community called Beverly Ridge being built on leveled mountain-tops just above the city of Beverly Hills.

On Tuesday afternoon O'Brien asked McDonald to send

Andrea Ordin in. The young lady attorney subsequently entered, wearing an exquisite beige dress. O'Brien watched admiringly as she seated herself opposite him, crossing her shapely panty-hosed legs. 'I didn't have time to talk with Eric Collins,' O'Brien said. 'What's with the art frauds?'

Andrea sighed. 'I was afraid you were going to ask me that,' she said. 'Let's say this case is a bagel of impotence surrounding a hole of frustration.'

'Not a bad figure of speech,' said O'Brien, 'but how so?'

'Well, let's put it this way,' said Andrea. 'We have two sets of casts of characters and you can't tell the good guys from the bad guys. On the one hand we have movie stars, industrialists, and even a big, rich California politician, whose name I'm sure is familiar to you. They buy up paintings to show off to their friends. Some of them have discovered the tax gimmick that if you buy a painting cheap, get it certified as an old master, and get a high appraisal on it, you can donate it to a museum or a college and take the full amount of the appraisal as a deduction on your income tax. That's what one customer, a well-known producer, had in mind when he tried to give the fake Rembrandt to the Bowers Museum. I'm sure *he* didn't know it was a fake and neither do most of these other jokers. The problem is that when we prove to them that their so-called works of art are forgeries or reconstructions, they don't want to admit to the world that they're idiots for being taken – or worse, that they may be playing games with the tax people. So we have no complainants. The only one who has the guts to testify is Gene Kelly, and the case against the guy who took *him* isn't too strong.'

'What about your second cast of characters?'

'Those are the guys who are preying on the vanity and the tax plans of the suckers. The same names keep popping up all the time. There's the Spanish count from the Rembrandt case. There's a doctor who has a hundred alleged old masters he claims to be worth millions of dollars, in his ratty little house in Woodland Hills. There's a travel agent who sells paintings on the side. There's a gallery owner on Sunset Boulevard who specializes in this junk. There's an eighty-five-year-old man, a former curator of a museum, who'll certify almost *anything* as an old master for a fee of twenty dollars. For twenty bucks he's gone as high as a million and a half dollars in his appraisals. And then there's a little Hungarian refugee who seems to work for the others when they need him. He's an art restorer. He can take any old painting out of someone's attic and make it look like a Utrillo or a Monet. He's not a bad painter on his own, so God knows *what* he's turning out back there in his studio.'

O'Brien said, 'Is this going on mostly down here in L.A. or is it statewide?'

Andrea replied, 'The nature of this town being what it is, the preponderance of the activity is down here. Just today Edward G. Robinson called to tell me someone wanted to sell him a collection from Düsseldorf, Germany. Claimed to have genuine Manets, Rubens, Michelangelos, and Breughels, no less. This is the center because everyone knows a good painting is a status symbol here, like an eleven millimeter pearl, but Eric Collins has had some stuff up North, too. Whether it emanates from L.A. or not, we don't know.

'In one of Eric's cases, a young couple from Telegraph Hill in San Francisco bought a good bad Utrillo at an auction by a legitimate dealer. It was authenticated on the back of a photograph of the painting by Lucy Valore, who was married to Utrillo when he died. The authentication ostensibly was in her handwriting. A funny thing, the dealer was shocked when the couple paid him five thousand dollars and then said they *didn't* want to donate it to a college.

'Anyway, the couple got suspicious when they read in the papers about our investigation and they ended up with Eric. Eric wrote to Paris, to a friend of his in the French Sûreté, and asked him to send a sample of Lucy Valore's handwriting. When it came in, he turned it over to our C.I.I. lab, along with the handwritten authentication on the back of the photograph. It didn't take our lab men more than two minutes to determine that the authentication was a fake, *not* in Lucy Valore's hand-writing. It followed, therefore, that the painting was a fake, too. We didn't have a case because the con man who consigned the Utrillo to the dealer left the state in a hurry. But the couple sued the dealer and he settled by giving them their five thousand dollars back.'

O'Brien tapped his fingers on the edge of his desk, thinking. His mind had gone back to something Andrea had said earlier. 'A Hungarian art restorer, eh?' he said, almost to to himself. Then, to Andrea, 'How would you like the C.I.I. to put Leroy Sana to work with you?'

Astounded, Andrea said, 'Leroy *Sana?* On a case like *this?*'

O'Brien nodded.

'I'll take him,' said Andrea.

But not yet was Andrea to acquire the crack agent.

The next morning, Wednesday, Miles Rubin, the Senior Assistant AG in charge of the office, was sitting at his desk, nibbling at his moustache and worrying about two things: pot smokers had been discovered in the school of his eleven-year-old daughter, Joni, and he knew that his wife, Renee, was going to hit him up for a new dress to wear at an American Jewish Committee affair the following week. He was moodily contemplating the latter eventuality when his intercom buzzed. It was Bea, his secretary.

Bea said, 'There's a man on the phone who insists on speaking to you and you alone. I don't know whether he's a nut or not.'

'Turn him over to whoever's on pixie duty,' Rubin grumbled. (Pixie duty is the chore of answering phone calls and in-person complaints from the public, assigned to the younger attorneys on a rotating basis, each serving one day per month.)

Bea said, 'I tried that, but he won't be put off. He says it has to be *you*.'

Rubin sighed. 'O.K.,' he said, 'I'll take the call.'

Rubin pressed one of the buttons on his phone and the man introduced himself as Thomas Devins. The name sounded faintly familiar to Rubin and he said, 'Go on. What can I do for you, Mr. Devins?'

Devins, obviously distraught, said, 'I'm calling you because your office is supposed to be the watchdog over other law enforcement agencies. Well, a couple of men in the District Attorney's office are trying to extort thirty-five thousand dollars out of me.'

'*What?*' exclaimed Rubin.

'Yes,' said Devins. 'They're investigating me for the mur-

der of a woman I was traveling with in Europe and she disappeared. My lawyer tells me they'll drop the investigation for thirty-five thou.' Then he added nervously, 'But I don't want to talk about it on the phone. Can't you meet me somewhere?'

Suddenly Rubin remembered where he had heard the name Devins. It was in his conversation a few weeks before with his friend in the DA's office, when he was told about the ex-parking lot attendant, Devins, who was with the wealthy Mrs. Norma Wilson in Europe when she vanished without a trace, and there was some mysterious connection with Moise Tshombe, the former Premier of the Congo.

Rubin said, 'I can't leave the office, Mr. Devins, but I can send one of our best special agents to talk with you. Where do you live?'

'No, not at my home or my office,' said Devins. 'Tell him to go to the coffee shop of the Continental Hyatt House at noon and ask for me.'

Rubin said, 'He'll be there.' He hung up and dialed Leroy Sana's extension. He told Sana what he just had heard on the phone and asked him to keep the noon appointment at the Continental Hyatt House. Sana said, 'But Charlie just put me on the art frauds case.'

'That'll hold,' said Rubin. 'This might be more urgent. I'll fix it with Charlie.'

Precisely at noon Sana walked into the lobby of the Sunset Boulevard hotel. He's a solidly built, balding man of about forty, with pale gray eyes and a face that reflects constant subdued grief over the chronic illness of his wife, Gloria. Before he came with the C.I.I., he put in eleven years as a sergeant-investigator in the Los Angeles County Sheriff's Department.

Sana went to the coffee shop and found Devins, an athletic-looking, expensively dressed, but extremely nervous young man. Sana gravely listened to Devins' story and arranged for him to come into the AG's office the next day to dictate a full report. Then Sana rushed back to see Rubin.

'This is hot stuff,' he told the Senior Assistant. 'It looks as if the bag-man is this guy's lawyer. He's one of those fancy Beverly Hills attorneys, name of Jerry Weber. You know him?'

Rubin's eyes widened. 'Sure I do,' he said. 'What's your plan?'

'I think we ought to wire Devins up with a miniature tape recorder and a miniature radio transmitter the next time he sees Weber, and let's find out from what Weber has to say whether Devins is bullshitting or not. Can you get Charlie's permission?'

Rubin went into O'Brien's office, just around the corner beyond the Xerox machines, and came back in less than five minutes.

'Permission granted,' he said.

On Thursday O'Brien had a long talk in his office with Gerard Shoemaker, agent-in-charge of the Bureau of Narcotic Enforcement in Los Angeles. The subject was the case of Unk and Squeak and the fifty weapons, including machine guns, which they wanted in trade for heroin.

'So this isn't just the run-of-the-mill heroin case?' said O'Brien.

'No,' said Shoemaker. 'These ass-holes – their real names are Robert Verstraeten and Richard Ramsaier, by the way – are peddling the guns to black and white militants. If some of *those* crazy bastards get hold of machine guns, there are going to be a lot of dead people in California.'

'O.K., then, what's your problem?'

'The machine guns. Where do we get them? From the National Guard maybe? Hand-guns we've got plenty of.'

'You mean you actually want to *give* them the guns?'

'Yeah, so we can make a good solid narcotics bust and put them away for a long time.'

O'Brien snapped his fingers. 'Say,' he said, 'we've got plenty of machine guns right here in the building. The C.I.I. took them from the Minute Men in a raid a couple of months ago. Nearly ran me down with them when they were taking them to the arsenal in the garage in the basement. That is, if you don't mind using right-wing machine guns.'

'Right wing, left wing,' shrugged Shoemaker. 'It's all in a day's work.'

On Friday Albert Harris told O'Brien he was going to present the Kirschke murder case to the Los Angeles Grand Jury on the following Tuesday, June 6th.

CHAPTER NINE

Preparations to go before a Grand Jury. Frenzy time in the prosecutor's office. Lining up potential witnesses. Interviewing them so their stories are fixed in their minds. Checking up on the attitudes of possible adversary witnesses.

Harris to Frice: 'Go to Yermo and check up on the attitude of Dennis Baily, the gas station attendant.'

Upon returning from Yermo, Frice to Harris: 'This kid is nineteen years old, blond, blue-eyed, the All-American-boy type. He always had made out pretty good with the chicks, but nothing like this ever happened to him before. Girls, some of them in XKE's and MG's and Mercedes, coming from as far away as Barstow just to look at a gas pump jockey in a service station out in the desert.

'Baily is a celebrity in Yermo, population nine hundred and fifty, and he knows it. He and Gene Ledet, who works with him nights at the gas station, collect L.A. newspaper headlines like "Two Gas Station Attendants Key Witnesses in Kirschke Murders." Baily reads every word about the case and considers himself an expert. He waits for the truck from Barstow to deliver the L.A. *Times* at five A.M. He picks up the L.A. *Herald-Examiner* as soon as it comes in. He goes to the library every day to read suburban papers like the *Valley Times* and the Long Beach *Independent*. He expresses his opinions of the reporters assigned to the case. He has told people he doesn't like Dial Torgerson of the *Times*, but he admires Bob Schmidt of the Long Beach papers because "he's very fair to Kirschke and must have covered all Kirschke's great cases as a DA right there in Long Beach."

'Baily tells everyone who will listen about what happened to him after the murders. He relates how Joe Carroll, Kirschke's private investigator, showed up a few days later and asked him if he remembered the red VW the morning of April ninth. He tells how Carroll asked him if he could identify Kirschke from a photograph, and how Kirschke himself then arrived with Carroll. He liked Kirschke and thought he was a very handsome man. He did not like our Barney Allen when he came to the station and asked him many of the same questions. He referred to Barney as "a different kind of fuzz, from the Attorney General." He never had heard of the Attorney General before.

'When he received our subpoena to testify before the Grand Jury, he acted as if it were the biggest thing that ever had happened to him in his life. He went around telling people that Bob Schmidt in the Long Beach *Press-Telegram* had written that the whole case might hinge on what he, Dennis Baily, had to say in his testimony.'

Fragments of conversation between Frice and his fellow C.I.I. agents: 'Sure the gas station boys are important, but I'm hung up on the gun. . . . The .38 caliber Harrington and Richards Defender, serial number 22068, owned by Kirschke. . . . Same make and caliber as the weapon that killed Elaine and Drankhan. . . . In a murder case where you don't have the weapon, you're in trouble. If you can't find it, the next-best thing is to learn if it ever was test-fired so you can check the ballistics against the markings on the death bullets. . . .

'I'm still looking for the gun. No *record* of it anywhere, either. . . . Not in the C.I.I. files in Sacramento. . . . Not in the police files in Los Angeles, Encino, Santa Monica, Long Beach, Burbank, Pasadena, Malibu, Anaheim. Nowhere. . . . Think I'll go over the records again. . . . I'm tracing the history of the gun again – from the Postal Inspectors all the way to David Weinstein of the United Sporting Goods store. . . .

'Weinstein. There was something he said that bothered me at the time . . . not bothered, just a vague feeling. . . . What the *hell* was it? . . .

'No time now. . . . Must get the witnesses lined up for the Grand Jury.'

CHAPTER TEN

In the public mind the Grand Jury is the least known and least understood link in the chain of law enforcement and the judicial process. It is, in a way, a mystery to most people because no one is allowed inside the walls of the Grand Jury room except the prosecutor and the witnesses. The press is forbidden to enter. Not even attorneys are permitted to be in the room with their clients while they are testifying. There is no judge.

So secret are the Grand Jury hearings that Rule 6 (e) of the Federal Rules of Procedure states that 'no person shall disclose the finding of an indictment,' except when necessary to issue and serve a warrant or a summons, and provides heavy fines and jail terms for violators. The reason for the secrecy is a built-in protection against unscrupulous prosecutors who might use unfounded charges in the Grand Jury to damage the reputations of innocent people whom they could not convict in court. The Grand Jury itself is a buffer against potential police-state measures. Its function is to screen out frivolous and groundless cases that a ruthless prosecutor might otherwise try to railroad into court for the purposes of, say, political persecution or revenge. It alone decides if the prosecutor's case has merit enough to be tried before a judge and a regular jury. If the Grand Jury decides that the prosecutor has *no* case, the secrecy of its deliberations protects the innocent from public scorn, contempt, obloquy, etc. (in the language of the statutes), and there is no trial.

Grand Juries have come under attack lately because they are composed mostly of wealthy retired people, the only ones who can afford to serve for a year or more, with very little remuneration. The contention is that in many cases the accused is not facing a panel of his peers. Also, a prosecutor, by hand-picking the members of his Grand Jury, occasionally can develop a captive body which will do anything he wants. This was the case, according to some critics, with District Attorney Jim Garrison in New Orleans. Most experts feel, however, that the Grand Jury system, with all its faults, is superior to anything else in the world. Charles O'Brien says, 'It *does* filter out the phony cases, and it *does* send the accused along the path to getting a fair trial in which his attorneys can assure a *real* jury of his peers by questioning and challenging the prospective veniremen.'

There are Federal Grand Juries, hearing the proposed cases of the United States Attorneys, and there are state Grand Juries serving each area in which a District Attorney operates – usually a county. Grand Juries vary in size. In California, for example, all counties, except Los Angeles, by law have nineteen-man Grand Juries. Los Angeles, because of the size of its population, has a twenty-three-man Grand Jury, with fourteen votes of the twenty-three necessary to indict.

The Los Angeles County Grand Jury meets in a wood paneled room which is, in effect, a wing of the District Attorney's office on the fifth floor of the Hall of Justice, just a block from the State Building which houses the Attorney General's Los Angeles staff. Unlike the granite pile of the Old State Building, which at least has clean Doric lines, the Hall of Justice is a rococo forbidding Victorian monstrosity, with its many jutting granite blocks providing roosting places for pigeons and starlings. On the top floor of the Hall of Justice are holding tanks for prisoners. Possibly because of these, plus the bird droppings, the Hall of Justice always seems to have a rank smell.

The Grand Jury Room, however, is immaculate and efficiently air conditioned. It is about fifty-by-thirty feet in size – no bigger than a large drawing room – and the Grand Jury members sit in individual chairs behind long desks, arranged in rows, amphitheater style. They face what looks like a judge's bench and a witness stand. The prosecutor and his assistants sit behind the bench.

This was the sight which greeted Albert Harris when he arrived, with Samoian, to present his case against Jack Kirschke to the Grand Jury on the morning of June 6th.

Harris nodded formally to the Grand Jury foreman, Lynne Frantz, and set about arranging his papers. When the jury members had settled down behind their desks, Frantz swore in the court reporter and abruptly began: 'Name of possible defendant: Jack Kirschke. Matters to be considered in connection with the above-named possible defendant: Alleged murder of Elaine Kirschke and Orville W. Drankhan.' Frantz then briefly related the circumstances of the alleged crime and asked that if any Grand Jury member had any 'state of mind which will prevent him from acting impartially and without prejudice,' he should now retire. No one retired.

Then Harris was introduced to the Grand Jury and told to begin calling his witnesses. Each witness, as he was called, was ushered to the door of the Grand Jury room by C.I.I. agents Byram, Frice, and Allen, from the corridor outside. The witness identified himself, was sworn in by Frantz 'to tell the truth, the whole truth, and nothing but the truth, so help you God,' and Harris immediately started his questioning.

In all, thirty-six witnesses were called, over a period of four days. Kirschke himself was *not* called. He had been invited to appear but had declined. He could not be subpoenaed or compelled to appear because under our system a defendant or possible defendant is protected by the United States Constitution from being forced to testify against himself or to be put in a position where he might inadvertently incriminate himself. Many accused persons nevertheless have chosen voluntarily to appear before Grand Juries and have succeeded in proving their innocence, thus preventing the action against them from ever getting to trial. Kirschke did not elect to do so.

One of the first witnesses to be called by Harris was James A. Miller, the young reserve Deputy Sheriff who is the son-in-law of Frank Cornell, the Kirschkes' upstairs neighbor. Using the stilted language of nearly all policemen when they testify, young Miller told how he had been visiting the Cornells on the weekend of the murder and had noted the absence of the habitual blaze of lights in the Kirschke apartment on Saturday night, April 8th.

Thinking this strange, Miller had waited until Sunday and then proceeded downstairs to check the Kirschke apartment. He observed that the doors were locked and then proceeded to look into one of the windows. He then observed, he said, the bodies of Elaine Kirschke and Bill Drankhan in the bedroom and notified the Long Beach police. How did he know they were dead? By their coloration, he said.

While he had him on the stand, Harris skillfully led Miller into testimony about the violent argument he had witnessed between Kirschke and his wife the preceding Christmas. The questioning went as follows:

Q: Would you tell us what you observed at that time?
A: I observed Mr. Kirschke with his back to me. He appeared to have Mrs. Kirschke up against the wall or the archway leading from the kitchen to the dining room and appeared to be striking her.
Q: Did you actually see him strike her?
A: Yes, sir, I did.

Out of the corner of his eye, Harris noticed several of the jurors exchange glances but he decided to let his prior pattern-of-violence theme drop for the time being, only to give it more dramatic impact when he brought it up again later. Instead, he called up considerable technical testimony from the police about the murder scene, how the bodies were found, where the bullets had penetrated, etc. Most of this was the necessary routine of murder presentations before Grand Juries, but Harris came up with an unexpected bonus when he had one policeman – Long Beach detective Garold E. McIntyre, no less – on the stand. McIntyre testified that Kirschke had taken at least two guns out of evidence in previous trials, 'a nine millimeter automatic and a .38 caliber revolver.' (For strategy reasons, Harris didn't make too much of the Harrington and Richards Defender before the Grand Jury, so he used McIntyre just to register the point that Kirschke did have weapons available to him.)

McIntyre said he couldn't find either gun when he searched the apartment after the murders, and then Harris abruptly switched the subject to the conversation McIntyre had had with Kirschke after he had been picked up by the police in Victorville, California, on his way back from Las Vegas on the Monday morning following the killings. It was McIntyre who took Kirschke home when he had been released in Victorville.

Q: Now, in driving from Victorville to Long Beach, did Mr. Kirschke make any comment?
A: Yes. Well, I couldn't quote him verbatim, but he said, 'I guess there goes my judgeship.'
Q: Did he make any comment indicating sorrow or remorse about his wife?
A: No, sir.

There was a noticeable shocked stirring among the jurors. Harris didn't know whether they were reacting to the judgeship comment or the lack-of-sorrow-and-remorse observation, but he made a note to himself to be sure to emphasize the unnatural callousness angle if the case ever got to trial.

Harris entered into evidence the tan knit sport shirt, worn by Kirschke, with its tiny bloodstains; and also the handwritten we'll-live-in-separate-bedrooms note by Elaine. Harris did not emphasize either because he knew they were open to challenge if Kirschke was indicted.

Harris then concentrated on tracing the chronology of the night of the murder. Kirschke, by his own admission to the police, left home in the Volkswagen at 7:30 that evening, stopped at Hof's Hut Marina where he bought some cigars and had a drink, and entered the Los Angeles International Airport parking lot at 8:26 P.M., according to the time stamped on his ticket. Harris brought in a witness from the parking lot to testify that no car that entered at 8:26 P.M. left later than 9:56 P.M. (Kirschke had told the police he waited at the airport until 11 P.M. before he left in the VW to drive to Las Vegas.)

In an attempt to convince the Grand Jury that instead of driving directly to Las Vegas, Kirschke had first gone home and had a confrontation with Elaine and Drankhan, Harris put a succession of witnesses on the stand. They were mainly neighbors who walked their dogs at night. The favorite local canine urination place, it seemed, was a large palm tree outside the Kirschke apartment. The Kirschkes did not have draperies on their windows, so it was easy to look inside while the dogs were relieving themselves. One of the dog waterers was Mrs. Lisette Avery, who stopped at the palm tree at about 11 P.M. on the night of the murders.

Q: Mrs. Avery, did you see anyone in the front room or the living room?
A: Yes, there was – let's see – as I would be looking in the window, to my right I could see the knees of someone.
Q: Did it appear to be a man?
A: Yes.
Q: And did it appear to be a stocky man?
A: Well, the reason I would say it was a man is because they were large knees and pants legs.
Q: Well, in any event, from what you saw you formed the opinion it was a stocky man?
A: Yes.
Q: Was it Jack Kirschke?
A: I at no time thought about Jack being there. Of course I didn't think about it very much.
Q: I understand that. But I am not asking you what you were thinking about, but when you looked in the room—
A: I did not see what I would recognize as Jack, no.
Q: Well, it was your impression that whoever it was in the living room was not Jack. Is that a fair statement?
A: Yes.
Q: And where was Elaine in the apartment?
A: Elaine was standing at the entrance to her kitchen. There is a cupboard there and I assume a draining board.
Q: Could you tell what she was doing, other than attending to something?
A: No. She just seemed to be bending over the drainboard, occupied with something.
Q: (With quiet emphasis) And could you see another person standing behind Elaine?
A: I saw somebody opening the cupboard door that was beyond her, yes.
Q: How much of that person could you see?
A: Arm.
Q: Just the arm?
A: Uh-huh.
Q: Could you tell that it was a man's arm?
A: Well, there was nothing that struck me about the arm that was rugged.

Q: It was a bare arm?
A: Bare arm.

(Harris previously had taken pains to inform the jury that Drankhan was a rugged two-hundred-pound man and that Kirschke is slender.)

Mrs. Avery testified that she couldn't hear any sounds of argument among the three people. But sixteen-year-old Christine Cornell, who lived upstairs, did. She heard loud voices, she said, between 10:30 and 11 P.M.

Shortly after 11 P.M., the next witness testified, Elaine and Drankhan arrived together at the Long Beach Yacht Club. The witness was Mrs. Margaret Janes, a waitress in the yacht club bar. She said that the couple drank heavily in the bar until about 1 A.M. when they left arm in arm.

Within a half hour, more or less, they were dead. Was Kirschke waiting for them back at the apartment? It was an unspoken question, but Harris did not have to make the point to the Grand Jury.

Having established his view of the chronology, Harris brought on the first of the openly pro-Kirschke witnesses – Joe Carroll, the private investigator hired by the accused Assistant District Attorney. Carroll was cool and professional on the stand. He straightforwardly repeated the timetable of his trip to Yermo in a 1963 Volkswagen and said confidently, 'This timetable definitely clears Mr. Kirschke.' The Grand Jury looked impressed. Harris sweated.

Harris decided to bring up a point he actually had wanted to defer – the fact that Kirschke knew about his wife's affair with Drankhan. He asked Carroll if he had worked for Kirschke before. Carroll said he had.

'When?'

'In January.'

'For what purpose?'

'To check out his wife's latest boy friend – Drankhan.'

'You mean you did this for Mr. Kirschke as a private investigator?'

'I did.'

'What was the purpose of the investigation?'

'Mr. Kirschke wanted to make sure the relationship wouldn't result in adverse publicity.'

The Grand Jury didn't look so impressed any more. Harris stopped sweating.

Next came the Jolly Girls. Harris preferred not to use them now, but he felt they had become necessary to bolster his prior-pattern-of-violence theme. The Jolly Girls – Pat Katz, Norma McIntire, and Marma Herfter – stirred up quite a reaction when they showed up in the corridor outside the Grand Jury room. It was there that the newspaper reporters clustered daily to pick up every crumb of information they could garner to indicate what was going on inside the secret chamber. The arrival of the Jolly Girls provided them with plenty of crumbs. The newspapermen photographed them together and singly; they talked to Kirschke's lawyer, Ramsey, about them; and they rushed out to the Long Beach Yacht Club to accrue juicy titbits about their reported peccancies.

The three middle-aged swingers, however, were good witnesses. They repeated almost verbatim the stories they had told the C.I.I. agents about Kirschke's physical attacks on Elaine, her cowering from him in the bushes, etc. They helped convey the strong impression that Kirschke was not as blasé about Elaine's affair with Drankhan as the mores of Naples society would indicate.

For example, Mrs. McIntire was even more forthright than Harris hoped she would be when she described the scene after the cowering-in-the-bushes incident:

Q: Did Elaine say anything to you when she got in the car?
A: She said Jack had beaten her and she was afraid of him and that she didn't want to stay at Pat's house because it was too close and he knew the house too well.
Q: Did she say anything to the effect that she had made a comment to Jack before she left the Kirschke house?
A: Yes. She said to him, 'Why don't you get a gun and shoot me?'

But as Harris long since had learned, a witness sometines can do serious damage and negate prior testimony by volunteering too much. He was trying to draw Mrs. McIntire out on Kirschke's knowledge of the Elaine-Drankhan affair, and he asked if Kirschke had ever said anything to her about it:

> A: Yes, he did. I thought it was very unusual for his attitude – and he said Elaine had worked hard all her life and she was over forty and might as well enjoy herself.

'Shit,' Harris murmured to Samoian after Mrs. McIntire was excused from the stand. 'Now the jury won't know whether or not Kirschke was really angry enough about Elaine's screwing around to kill her.'

Nevertheless, Harris made the instant judgment that, on the whole, the Jolly Girls testimony – added to the threats and violence overheard by the upstairs neighbors – was effective. He decided to hold back a crucial witness he had been keeping in reserve – Kirschke's secretary, Sharon Lyle.

While all this was going on, the two gas station boys, Dennis Baily and Gene Ledet, were hanging around in the corridor outside. They were enjoying themselves immensely. They granted interviews to the press, though they were careful not to discuss their impending testimony, as they had been warned. They chatted gaily with the other witnesses. They even talked with the Jolly Girls, after seemingly resenting, at first, the emergence of the ladies as co-celebrities in the case. Although no one realized it at the time, these corridor conversations between the gas station boys and the Jolly Girls were to become vitally important later on.

Harris got the gas station boys on and off the witness stand in a hurry. Baily, visibly nervous in the sterile wood-paneled atmosphere, positively remembered Kirschke's red, rusted, dented Volkswagen pulling in for gas sometime between 2:30 and 4 A.M. on the night of the murders. Under Harris's questioning, the youth admitted he had not been able to identify Kirschke when he showed up at the gas station a week later, but that he was pretty sure it was the same man who had been driving the VW. Ledet, equally nervous, confirmed Baily's story. He was a little more vague than Baily about the time the VW had driven into the station, but he said that when he saw Kirschke later, 'the face looked familiar.'

After the two youths were excused, Samoian heaved a sigh of relief and said, 'Well, they didn't hurt us too much.'

'We'll see,' said Harris.

Harris finished his presentation to the Grand Jury on June 11th. On June 14th, a Friday, the Grand Jury assembled in the courtroom of Superior Court Judge Robert Feinerman. The judge asked Foreman Lynne Frantz if he had an indictment to present to the court. Frantz said, 'Yes, I do, Your Honor.' He handed a copy of the indictment to the bailiff. The judge read the indictment and asked Frantz if fourteen or more members of the Grand Jury had voted to return it. 'Yes, they did, Your Honor,' said Frantz.

'Then the court finds the indictment to be a true bill,' said Judge Feinerman, 'and a bench warrant is issued for the apprehension of the defendant.'

Kirschke now was officially charged with two counts of murder in the first degree, with the trial date to be set later.

The judge turned to Harris, who was in the courtroom, and asked, 'Is this a death penalty case?'

Harris said, 'It is, Your Honor.'

The judge said, 'All defendants must be treated the same by this court, so there will be no bail.'

That afternoon Kirschke was suspended from his post as Assistant District Attorney. He was arrested and taken in handcuffs to the Hall of Justice, where he was put in a cell in the holding tanks on the top floor. As he entered the building where he had started his career as a prosecutor eleven years before, he smiled and waved his handcuffed hands at the crowd. He told the press, 'I never did like this building. It's grim and forbidding.' He also predicted he would be completely exonerated.

Kirschke's attorney, Albert C. S. Ramsey, had a few words for the press, too. He said, 'Harris so twisted and distorted the case before the Grand Jury as to make it unrecognizable.' Ramsey was extremely bitter about District Attorney Evelle Younger's suspension of Kirschke from his duties as an Assistant DA, even though he was in jail. 'That,' said Ramsey, 'was a Mickey Mouse action.'

In the Attorney General's office, just down the street, O'Brien was discussing the Grand Jury proceeding with an ebullient Samoian and an exhausted Harris. Samoian said, 'Well, Al's gamble sure worked. If the Grand Jury believed us, even with Kirschke's witnesses, then the trial jury will believe us.'

Harris was too tired to answer his young colleagues. O'Brien said gently, 'This is a nine-inning ball game and all we've done is gotten through our half of the first inning with a very weak batting order. The other side hasn't even come to bat yet.'

Since it was Friday afternoon, O'Brien left the review of the case fairly early in order to fly home to see his son, Devin. Devin was back home now and out of the wheelchair, but he was still limping badly. Also the doctors continued to be uncertain about the reproductive organ problem. Devin's weight had increased alarmingly from seventy pounds to more than a hundred.

That afternoon C.I.I. agent Gene Frice, too, had to rush to the airport. His Green Beret unit had been called to active duty. He was about to parachute into the Big Delta wilderness north of Fairbanks, Alaska. His unit had to practice organizing the Eskimos and Indians into insurgency guerrilla groups while the entire Alaskan Command – playing the part of an invading occupying foreign power – tried to hunt them down and destroy them.

It would be weeks before Frice could turn his attention once again to the vexing problem of the Harrington and Richards Defender, Serial Number 22068.

CHAPTER ELEVEN

Another premature heat wave hit Los Angeles. The shoppers on Sixth Street and on Wilshire Boulevard clung to the scant shade of the sidewalk awnings as they scampered from one air-conditioned emporium to another, like bait-worms evading the fisherman's flashlight. The parasols blossomed – scattered colored mushrooms over the heads of old ladies venturing into the sun-blistered avenues near their retirement cottages in the back streets of Hollywood and Burbank. Mini-skirted movie-studio tour guides brought sunburn lotion to work with them. At night the hot desert air flowing over the still-cold Pacific caused fingers of fog to reach inland as far as Beverly Hills and Culver City. In the morning the sun slapped the fingers away again.

In the Old State Building at Spring and First Streets, the ancient air-conditioning system once again wheezed its lukewarm currents into the cubicles that delineated the many units of the Attorney General's office. Each unit or team was made up of a group of lawyers, investigators, or both, working on their own specific cases. O'Brien had helped perfect the microcosm structure and was proud of it. He had the legal authority, the personnel, and the money to operate this way, and he was the envy of other state attorneys general when he occasionally conferred with them at meetings, as a stand-in for Lynch. New York's Louis Lefkowitz, for example, once told O'Brien he was so limited in money and power that his comparatively few investigations and legal actions required constant remobilization of his personnel.

O'Brien didn't have to worry about that.

While the unit handling the Kirschke murder case was reaching a climax of activity in the Grand Jury hearings, the other units kept doing their own thing, each insulated from each other, yet remotely interconnected, like the cells of a living body.

Typically, Andrea Ordin, in her own unit, was barely aware of what was going on in the Kirschke case – except for what she read in the newspapers. Occasionally when she consulted with O'Brien in his office, she'd drop into the Harris command post in Lynch's office just down the hall, but she'd chat only briefly with Harris and Samoian before they turned back to their accordion files. There weren't many of the usual places for intermicrocosm gossip. The Redwood Restaurant across the street was where many of the AG's people had lunch, but it also was frequented by cops and politicians from the neighboring Police Headquarters and City Hall, and it was too noisy, and there were too many prying ears, for the discussion of confidential matters.

There also was the bedraggled cafeteria on the roof of the Old State Building, but the bad food and coffee made it impossible to concentrate on anything else but its ingestion.

Another meeting place for the various units was the office of C.I.I. agent Mike Serio who specialized in pornography cases and always had plentiful exhibits of his most recent raids. Many young male attorneys frequently congregated there.

Like all the others, Andrea had six or seven cases going at the same time. Every week she wound up one or two, and one or two new ones were dropped on her desk. Some, like the school integration cases, were major projects and consumed months of her attention. Others came and went quickly. While the Kirschke case was before the Grand Jury, for example, she was more or less marking time on the art frauds puzzle, and she concentrated on the matter of the People of the State of California vs. The Nancy Nolan Employment Agency.

The Nancy Nolan agency was suspected of two violations of state law. First, they allegedly were committing fraud by advertising jobs which didn't exist. It was a ploy to get girls in to register with the agency and fill out applications. The second charge was even more disturbing to Andrea, a devout liberal who had campaigned vigorously against Proposition Fourteen (a proposed constitutional amendment to overturn a ban on racial discrimination in housing in California) and who, long after the measure had been voted down by the people, still had a Proposition Fourteen campaign poster resolutely tacked up in her office. Andrea suspected that in some undetermined way the Nancy Nolan agency was discriminating flagrantly against black and Mexican-American job applicants – in violation of the state's equal-opportunity Unruh Act.

The fraud charge was easy to pin down. The nonexistent jobs remained nonexistent when Andrea asked Nancy Nolan for proof of their validity. The discrimination allegation was more difficult to prove. It required undercover agents, and the C.I.I. did not at that time have lady investigators.

So Andrea organized her own corps of female agents to pose as applicants for secretarial jobs, in which Nancy Nolan specialized. Andrea recruited several of the many black and Mexican-American secretaries in the AG's office, gave them a brief course in undercover techniques, and sent them to apply for specific jobs advertised by Nancy Nolan in the newspapers.

Andrea had trained them well. The Negro and Mexican ladies all noticed that when they were interviewed by Nancy Nolan personnel, the number '9' always was typed on their application cards. None was sent out for the job she had applied for. Next, Andrea dispatched other AG secretaries – this time white ones – to apply for the same jobs. There was no '9' on the white girls' cards at the agency, and all were offered jobs.

Andrea subpoenaed the cards and had the '9's' and the non-'9's' lined up in neat piles in front of her on her desk. Then she phoned the Nancy Nolan people and asked them to come to her office for a conference. After having been served the subpoenas, the Nancy Nolanites apparently knew what was coming and entered meekly. There was no argument. They agreed almost immediately to sign a consent judgment to cease and desist from fraudulent and discriminatory practices. They also were fined $20,000.

Almost miraculously other Southern California employment agencies which quite possibly were using similar practices ceased and desisted from indulging in them.

While this and the Kirschke hearings were going on, the unit assigned to tracing the peregrinations of Father Nikliborc had acquired a new member. This was veteran C.I.I. agent Junell Diemel, who equipped himself with salt tablets as an antidote to the heat and took off into the desert to pick up the trail where charitable trust investigator John Fiscus had left off. He soon found more than the heat to disconcert him. Someone else was on the trail, too. Wherever he went, he learned that an agent of the U.S. Government's Internal Revenue Service had been there first. It didn't take long for Diemel to determine that the agent was Fred Nielsen, one of the IRS's finest.

The men working on Unk and Squeak and the deal to trade guns for heroin kept active on other cases while they awaited word from the Ventura County Sheriff's office that the contact had been made to consummate the deal.

One day during the Kirschke hearings (of which they too, were barely aware) the eight agents of Field Supervisor George Houston's team spent the good part of a morning going over the Unk–Squeak case at their desks in a large bullpen in the Bureau of Narcotic Enforcement office on the second floor of the Old State Building. Each agent had his own desk and telephone. The desks were side by side in the bullpen and backed up against each other, to utilize every inch of space in the room, which also was used by two other eight-man BNE teams. Although the men were mostly in their twenties, nearly every desk bore a photograph of a wife and children. There also were signs such as 'Peanut Butter Is Better than Pot' and 'Raise Poppies for Fun and Profit.'

There were Oriental, Mexicans, whites, and blacks. Long-haired and casually dressed, they were distinguished from any comparable group of graduate college students only by the small snub-nosed .38's they wore in their belts. Two members of the team, John Fairburn and Bruce Smith, were trainees – just out of college and on a year's probation (after their basic instruction in firearms, drugs, and such) before they became full-fledged agents. Fairburn wore thick eyeglasses and looked about eighteen. He and Smith were the butts of all humor. They also were required to go to the cafeteria to fetch coffee and sweet rolls for the others. In the field, however, they operated the same as anyone else, except that one of the more experienced agents generally looked after them.

The agents chatted about matters like subpoenas, suspects, and violations of rights. Intruding on their conversation was the constant drone of voices from a speaker in the room. These were other BNE agents, out in the field on cases, talking to each other and to the headquarters over the private radio channel that could not be monitored by anyone else – even other law enforcement agencies. The agents in the bullpen were acclimated to keep a fraction of their attention affixed to the voices on the speaker. The first hint of an emergency or a crisis – a suspect with a gun, for instance – would send them scurrying to their unmarked cars in the basement garage.

At 11:15 Houston, their field supervisor, emerged from his private office. Houston, a thin, balding man resembling a book-keeper, had been one of the best narco agents in the state for more than twenty years and the men knew it and they felt more secure when he was with them in the field. Houston brought out copies of the records of Unk, Robert Dean Verstraeten; and Squeak, Richard William Ramsaier. The agents all studied the Xeroxed documents.

Verstraeten was twenty-eight years old, six feet tall, weighed two hundred pounds, had blue eyes and brown hair a two-inch scar on the side of his neck, and hypodermic marks on both forearms, indicating that he was a heroin addict. His 'rap sheet,' or arrest record, was three pages long. It began when he was picked up for curfew violations when he was teen-ager, and graduated to charges of burglary, battery, car theft, and possession of narcotics. He had served two terms in prison.

Ramsaier's record was less revealing. The agents' reports indicated that he was twenty-six years old, six feet four inches tall, two hundred and twenty pounds, with blond hair and blue eyes, and with tattoos on both arms and hands. His occupation was listed as nurseryman. He had no needle marks on his arms. His 'rap sheet' showed only one previous arrest, for possession of narcotics.

'This is the dangerous one,' Roger Livingston muttered. 'He's smarter.'

'Why?' asked one of the younger agents.

'Because,' said Sixto Ramirez, the other senior agent, 'he doesn't get caught.'

Just then there was an interruption. Ramirez had been

trying to contact a Negro heroin peddler named Willie Jackson to make a buy of $3,500 worth of 'smack.' Now Jackson was phoning back, asking for 'Sands,' an undercover name used by Ramirez.

The eight agents and Houston silently moved into a soundproofed room that was equipped with a telephone, a tape recorder, and a speaker so the others could hear. Ramirez picked up the phone, and amazingly his voice switched easily to a Caribbean Negro accent.

Ramirez said, 'This is Sands.'

Jackson's voice said, 'I don't know what the mother-fuckin' hell is goin' on, but my connection got busted. I got no stuff.'

Ramirez said, 'Man, you got a leak somewhere.'

Jackson said, 'The old man brought the mother-fuckin' man to our house and eight got busted at the Chateau Motel. But tell you what I can do. I got another mother-fuckin' connection, and I can go there myself tomorrow. I'll take a trip and meet you anywhere in Vegas if you let me know where you're at.'

Ramirez: 'I move from motel to motel. How about meeting me here at the L.A. airport?'

Jackson: 'O.K., you call me tomorrow night at about seven-thirty and we'll set it up for Wednesday. I don't want to fuck you around.'

Ramirez: 'You know how I like to deal – clean, early, when there's no heat and I don't have to walk around with the shit in the street.'

Jackson: 'O.K., you call me tomorrow and I'll have the mother-fuckin' shit on Wednesday.'

Ramirez: 'O.K., but remember, I want no one there. I want to deal with you. Nobody else. And make sure it's a full pound this time for the thirty-five hundred. Last time it was short.'

Jackson: 'Maybe I made a mistake weighing it out. I'll make it up this time. I won't fuck you around.'

Ramirez: 'O.K. I'll call you tomorrow night then. And take care, brother. I don't want to lose *you*.'

Jackson: 'O.K. Tomorrow night.'

Ramirez hung up and he and the others filed out. They knew

that on Wednesday, Sands, 'a big smack dealer from Las Vegas,' hopefully would meet Jackson somewhere at the Los Angeles International Airport. Hopefully, Jackson would hand Ramirez a pound of heroin in exchange for $3,500 in marked state funds, and hopefully the other seven members of the team would be able to move in for a quick and peaceful arrest.

The agents went back to their desks.

'A couple of other things about Unk and Squeak,' Houston said. 'We've got to bust them before next Friday. On that day there's going to be one of those big public relations roundups of pushers and hypes to make the local police departments look good. If we don't rip Squeak and Unk before then, they'll get scared and go to ground.'

'What's the other thing you forgot to tell us, George?' Livingston asked.

'Oh, yes. Squeak and Unk always are armed. Squeak keeps saying he'll kill any pig who tries to bust him.'

The team handling the Devins case was now being led by Richard Huffman, a Deputy Attorney General normally handling organized crime cases. Before sending a bugged and wired Devins for a meeting with Weber, on which the C.I.I. agents would eavesdrop to check Devins' charge that Weber was attempting extortion, Huffman decided to discuss the case with O'Brien and Miles Rubin.

O'Brien said to Rubin, 'You have good contacts in the DA's office. Do they have any kind of case against this guy Devins?'

Rubin said, 'I don't know. Some of it is pretty weird. They say Devins was involved in a plot to spring Moise Tshombe – you know, the former premier of the Congo – from jail in Algeria. Devins is supposed to have gotten a million dollars somewhere to bribe the Algerian guards and fly Tshombe to the island of Majorca, off the coast of Spain. There must be some truth to this because Devins was dealing, at one time, with Luis Kutner, a lawyer who represented Mrs. Tshombe before the United Nations. Devins tried to get the money from Kutner but couldn't. He played like he was a secret agent. Used the code name "The Fox," and a lot of shit like that.'

O'Brien said, 'But how did Mrs. Wilson get mixed up in this James Bond stuff?'

Rubin said, 'I don't think she *was*. In fact, I don't know how she got mixed up with Devins in the first place.'

'I can answer that,' said Huffman. 'This Mrs. Wilson is fifty-seven years old, the daughter of a wealthy engineer, and married to a guy named William Wilson, who's fifteen years younger. She met Devins when he was about twenty years old. He was a kid from Arkansas and working as a parking lot attendant. She put him in charge of her real estate properties and he ended up managing the Brentwood Convalescent Home and an office building she owns on La Cienega Boulevard, both valued in the millions. He also ended up with fancy clothes and cars and a forty-eight-foot yacht. This kid still is only thirty years old.'

Rubins said, 'Hmmm. Then maybe she *was* involved in this Tshombe plot. Devins *did* get the money from somewhere.'

O'Brien said, 'Stop speculating. Just tell me what you were able to find out in the DA's office.'

'Well,' said Rubin. 'They know that Devins did a lot of fooling around in North Africa, talking to contacts and such. Then he came back to L.A. and flew to Montreal with an accomplice, a kid named Robert Forget – it's French and pronounced four-jay – who was his carpenter at the La Cienega office building. Mrs. Wilson met them in Montreal and Forget told the DA's people there were a lot of financial discussions. He got the idea Mrs. Wilson felt Devins was screwing her financially, but Devins convinced her he needed a lot of money from a real estate deal to get European backing for the Tshombe caper, from which he would realize ten million dollars.

'Anyway, Forget says Mrs. Wilson signed over the convalescent home to Devins and all three flew to Madrid. From Madrid they went to Tangiers, where Forget cut out. He says Devins told him he was now so snarled up financially with Mrs. Wilson that he'd have to kill her before they proceeded with the Tshombe plan. Forget says he didn't want any part of murder and flew back to the United States. So Devins and Mrs. Wilson went on alone to Zurich. They left Zurich by auto to drive to Geneva over wild mountainous roads. There's no sign that Mrs. Wilson ever arrived in Geneva. Devins did. The DA has a record of his checking in, by himself, at the Richemond Hotel. Devins says he left Mrs. Wilson at the International Hilton when they got to Geneva and that she was going to stay with old friends. In any event, no one has seen her alive since she and Devins left Locarno on their way from Zurich to Geneva.'

Huffman whistled softly to himself. 'Maybe this joker *is* guilty,' he said.

O'Brien roared, 'That's the DA's problem. Let *him* worry about it. Guilty or not, our job – as guardian of the guardians – is to find out if this attorney Weber and anyone in the DA's office could be playing some illegal games of their own.'

CHAPTER TWELVE

The continuing unrelenting heat contributed to an epidemic of testiness in the Los Angeles area. Albert Harris, preparing night and day for the start of the Kirschke trial, became testy with his wife Ursula when she complained that he wasn't even coming home weekends any more to see her and their three children. O'Brien was testy because his son, Devin, now hobbling about at home, continued to gain weight and was up to 130 pounds, increasing the possibility that he was becoming eunuchoid. Jack Kirschke was testy, even though he had been granted the use of a telephone, a desk, and the law library in the county jail, in order to help prepare his defense for the impending trial. Too many other inmates were badgering Kirschke to assist in *their* cases.

The testiest of all, perhaps, was C.I.I. agent Leroy Sana, who spent an afternoon cooking in his own private furnace in Beverly Hills. The furnace was an automobile, state-issue, an unmarked tan two-door Ford sedan. All the windows of the car were closed, and as the sun beat down on the metal roof, the 98-degree temperature outside soared to at least twelve degrees higher inside. Sana had to keep the windows closed so he and fellow-agent Barney Allen could concentrate on the sound of voices emanating from a tiny radio receiver on the seat beside him. A tape-recorder also was plugged into the radio receiver, and slowly spinning spools were making permanent capture of the voices.

The voices were those of Thomas Devins and the lawyer, Jerome Weber. Devins and Weber were conversing in Weber's office, across the street from where the C.I.I. car was parked, at 315 South Beverly Drive. Devins, in effect, was a miniature radio station. The transmitter, slightly larger than a pack of king-size cigarettes, was in his shirt pocket. The antenna ran over his shoulder, was taped to his body, and then extended down the inside of his trouser leg.

Earlier that day (as he had done once before when Devins was to meet with Weber) Sana had taken Devins to an unobtrusive-looking establishment on West Jefferson Boulevard known as SAC Electronics. There, in a back room, a police-systems expert named Anderson had asked Devins to strip and he wired him up with the miniature radio transmitter. Working with experienced thoroughness, Anderson also fitted an equally tiny tape recorder, called an EDI, in a back pocket of Devins' pants. Two wires extended from the EDI recorder to minuscule microphones pinned inside either side of Devins' jacket. Thus, Devins was outfitted with a pair of fail-safe, wholly independent mechanisms. The transmitter would send voices through the air to the receiver and tape recorder in the C.I.I. automobile; the EDI would be recording the same conversations on Devin's person. The EDI was locked and tamperproof, so its evidence could be presented legally in court. Its tape could not be erased or altered in any way, and it could be unlocked only with an 'allen wrench,' smaller than a jeweler's instrument, prior to replaying in Grand Jury proceedings or in court.

It was now up to Devins to prove the story he had told Huffman and Sana. According to Devins, he had returned to Los Angeles after Mrs. Wilson's disappearance during their African-European expedition, and he had found himself being dogged by a determined young investigator in the District Attorney's office, William Burnett. When Burnett made it clear to him that he suspected him of murdering Mrs. Wilson, Devins asked his attorneys to recommend a criminal lawyer. They suggested Jerome Weber and Devins became a Weber client.

As Devins had recounted the story, Weber made it clear early on that he had close connections among the investigators' staff of the Los Angeles County District Attorney's office. To prove it, he showed Devins a four-page confidential report written by Burnett about Devins' suspected involvement in Mrs. Wilson's suspected murder. The report was secret and not supposed to leave the DA's office. Weber later identified his sources as the chief of the DA's Bureau of Investigation, and a senior detective in the Bureau. To indicate further the cuddly nature of his relationship with these two, Weber gave Devins the details of an interrogation of his fellow suspect, Robert Forget, by Burnett, in Sedro Woolley, Washington, more than a thousand miles away. The senior detective had accompanied Burnett to Washington. The very next morning Weber knew everything that had transpired.

Finally, according to Devins, Weber suggested to him that he had arranged for him to take out an 'insurance policy.' The 'policy' would make it certain that Burnett would be shifted off the case and that Burnett's superiors 'would place the case in the inactive file and would not assign another investigator to it.' Weber said the money would be divided 'among his friends,' and that because of his connections in the District Attorney's office, 'this was a service that he made available to all his clients.'

At first Weber had told Devins the 'policy' would cost from four to six thousand dollars. Two weeks later, however, Weber informed Devins that he had checked with his friends, that the 'policy' *was* available, that it 'would include Grand Theft and Murder One,' but that the price would be thirty-five thousand dollars. He said that the senior detective's work in Sedro Woolley – providing Weber and Devins with confidential information about Burnett's interrogation of Forget – was worth five thousand dollars alone.

Devins had agreed to pay the thirty-five thousand dollars for the 'policy' – but it was then, after a month of stalling, that he had come to the Attorney General's office to tell his story.

Now wired up with the secret transmitter and tape recorder, he was discussing the 'policy' again with Weber in his office – while Sana and Allen listened in their car across the street. This was the second time he had visited Weber with the EDI recorder in his pocket. This time, however, he also had money with him to consummate the payoff. The money, wrapped up in four neat packages by Sana earlier in the day, actually consisted of only $6,750 cleverly assembled with blank sheets of money-sized paper to look like $35,000. The conversation in Weber's office referred only sporadically to the packages of money.

Sana, mopping the streaming perspiration from his face every few seconds, concentrated only on *those* fragments of the meandering dialogue between the two disembodied voices issuing from the radio receiver. He heard:

WEBER: You've got to shit or get off the pot. . . . If you

want me to do it, give me the loot and let me go to work....

DEVINS: Let me ask you something. Dumb question. Have they ever failed to come through? Have they ever taken any bread and then that's it?

WEBER: Oh, no, no. Never in a million years. Never.

DEVINS: If I back out now, I'm definitely going to be indicted?

WEBER: Oh, yeah. And if I didn't think so, I wouldn't let you make this deal.... You understand what I'm flirting with, I could be disbarred . . . I don't know that they're not being taped....

Sana couldn't suppress a grin as he mopped his face and looked over at Allen. 'So he thinks *they're* being taped,' he said. The voices kept rumbling from the radio receiver in the sweltering car:

WEBER: If you do it this way, it would be over with by Monday or Tuesday.

DEVINS: Right. . . . I – you know – not that I don't have assets. I have assets, but I'm not liquid.

WEBER: They *know* what you've got. All I know is what I submitted. I was a relay boy. If we negotiate and it's in an envelope, you know what I mean ... I wanted the service and I got it. Period....

DEVINS: Okay, you ...

WEBER: (Laughter) ... Tom, you're beautiful. I'll tell you. You are beautiful.... All mine?

Sana said to Allen, 'By God, he's given him the money.' Allen said, 'Sh,' and bent his ear closer to the receiver.

DEVINS: All yours.... I feel poor again....

WEBER: Well, ah, I don't know what I would have done in your spot. . . . Let me give you a five-minute speech. . . . Get that fucking money away from you before you change your mind.

DEVINS: No, it's here. Don't you worry about that.

The conversation drifted off into a discussion of legal technicalities, other Weber cases, and the political situation

in the Congo. As he listened, Sana became more and more agitated. Soon he was fuming inwardly as well as outwardly. He said to Allen, 'The fucking idiot is doing everything wrong. Before he gave Weber the money he was supposed to ask for another confidential memo on his case, signed by someone in the DA's office. Or to get the name of whoever gave Weber that first memo. Or to insist on speaking to the guy on the phone. Or to be present when the money was turned over to the DA's man hand-to-hand.'

Allen said, 'Hold it. Listen to this.'

Weber abruptly has asked his secretary to place a phone call to the District Attorney's office. During the pause, while Weber awaited completion of the call, Sana and Allen heard Devins say, 'Tell him the deal.' Then, over Weber's loudspeaker phone:

WEBER: Chief?
VOICE: Yes.
WEBER: Jerry Weber. How are you, Chief?
VOICE: Good.
WEBER: Say, I have a client.
VOICE: Yeah.
WEBER: Mr. Tom Devins.
VOICE: Yeah.
WEBER: You guys wanted to get his statement, right?
VOICE: Right.
WEBER: All right, I'll bring him down there at four-thirty on Wednesday.
VOICE: Four-thirty Wednesday?
WEBER: Right. . . . Only in the spirit of cooperation, sir.
VOICE: Good.
WEBER: But that's as far as it goes, sir.
VOICE: Okay.
WEBER: Thank you.
VOICE: You bet.
WEBER: Good-bye.

That was the end of the phone conversation. Sana and Allen heard Devins laugh and say, 'Beautiful! Spirit of co-operation!' But then the conversation drifted off again into extraneous matters. Sana groaned. He said to Allen, 'I'd better talk to this silly bastard.' He got out of the car and walked into the medical building at 300 South Beverly Drive, where he had once investigated a diet doctor for malpractice – first looking longingly at the cool haven of the Hamburger Hamlet up the street. He found a phone booth and dialed Weber's office. He said, 'This is Mr. Gould. I understand Mr. Tom Devins is in with Mr. Weber. Could I speak with him, please?'

Devins came on the phone. He knew that 'Mr. Gould' was the code name to be used in an emergency. Sana said, 'Can you talk?' Devins said, 'Yeah. Weber's in another room with a client.'

Sana said, 'Where's the fuckin' money?'

'He put it in his jacket pocket in his closet.'

Sana said, 'Well, you better figure out some kind of excuse and get your ass down here to talk to us.'

A few minutes later, Devins met Sana and Allen in the lobby of Weber's office building. Sana said angrily, 'You never even asked him about the report.'

Devins said, 'I did. I brought it up. You just don't know his attitude.'

Sana said, 'Well, there's only one thing you've got to do now. Go up there and get the money back.'

Devins said, 'It's impossible without tipping him off.'

Sana, still furious, replied, 'Well, then, I'm going to make the pinch on Weber now. At least we have a case on *him*.'

Devins said, 'No, don't. Then we'll never know whether there was a deal or not. Maybe when I go down to talk to the DA's people on Wednesday . . . '

Allen said, 'No, go back and get the money and we'll try again. If he's still out of his office, just take it out of his coat pocket. If he catches you, act like you're counting it.'

Devins pleaded for a while but then acceded and went back upstairs. About a half hour later, pale and shaken, he came down again – with the four packages of money. He had had no trouble retrieving the cash, but Weber, rushing to a client in another office, had seen him counting it. Devins then had slipped out on the pretext of getting a newspaper to read while waiting for Weber to complete his other business.

Sana asked Devins, 'Does our friend Weber have a regular place where he goes at night?'

Devins said, 'Yes, the Friars Club.'

Sana said, 'Well, phone him and try to make a date to see him there tonight. Tell him you took the money back and you want to talk with him again because he got you confused this morning about just how effective the "policy" would be. Tell him the phone call to the chief didn't mean enough to you. Okay?'

'Okay,' said Devins glumly.

Sana removed the locked miniature tape recorder from Devins' pocket and gave it Allen for safekeeping. Then the two agents dismissed Devins and went to lunch at the Hamburger Hamlet. 'It's a shame we have to do this all over again at the Friars Club tonight,' said Allen. 'And you were going to take Gloria to the doctor tonight, too.'

Sana shrugged. 'One of the kids will have to take her,' he said.

As they munched their super-hamburgers in the welcome cool of the plush ground-meat palace, their mien and their conversation was just as matter-of-fact as the accountants at the next table who had had a routine morning with their ledger books and adding machines.

CHAPTER THIRTEEN

The next day O'Brien arrived at his Los Angeles office and was observed to be in an exceedingly grumpy mood. His secretary, Muriel Duncan, heard him swearing in his private washroom and informed Executive Assistant Tom McDonald that though the heat wave had broken during the night, another kind of rough weather possibly was pending.

McDonald sauntered into the Chief Deputy's office just as O'Brien came out of the washroom, adjusting his pants. 'What's the matter, Charlie,' McDonald said, 'the Lo-Tel Motel getting you down?'

'No, goddamit,' bellowed O'Brien. 'I didn't *stay* at the Lo-Tel last night. Marie's coming down to see a play at the Mark Taper Forum, so I stayed at the Biltmore. I wouldn't pay them three-fifty for breakfast, so I ate at some greasy spoon joint down the street. A goddam disagreeable meal. The scrambled eggs were burned, and when I told the Mexican counterman in Spanish, "*Muy chocolate* – too brown," the goddam fool gave me a chocolate-covered doughnut.'

O'Brien's mood did not improve after he had read the reports brought to him by McDonald. One of them was from Sana, forwarded through Richard Huffman, and it dealt with the taping, the day before, of the conversations between Thomas Devins and Jerome Weber. Devins had met Weber again at the Friars Club in the evening, but the dialogue did nothing more to pin down the identity of Weber's alleged colleagues-in-bribery on the DA's investigative staff. Weber, in fact, was getting more and more suspicious of Devins' repeated questioning and at one point even had attempted to frisk Devins to see if he was bugged. Devins had escaped detection by making a joke of it. He had pulled back his suit jacket, carefully holding both hands over the two microphones, and had said, 'Go ahead and search me.' Weber then had made just a few desultory passes at his side pockets and subsided.

O'Brien grumbled, 'I *hate* these goddam electronic eavesdropping devices – especially in the hands of amateurs.'

McDonald said, 'But they're legal in this state. I remember when you went to the legislature . . . '

O'Brien glowered and McDonald thought it prudent not to finish the sentence. O'Brien resumed reading the reports. The Chief Deputy looked up and said, 'Goddamit, why can't everything be nice and clear-cut around here, the way it is in fiction?'

Suppressing a smile, McDonald said, 'You been reading crime novels again?'

O'Brien said, 'Yeah. I sat up half the night finishing a Ross McDonald. No relation?'

The Executive Assistant shook his head.

O'Brien continued: 'Damn good writing, but here's this private detective, Lew Archer, and he goes around tying up all the loose ends neatly, and everything turns out right. There are good guys and bad guys. The prosecutors all are righteous and the defense attorneys all are dedicated. You never need a scorecard to tell the players, if you're used to reading this stuff, like I am. But *here* – here we have an art frauds case where everybody is screwing everybody else. We have a priest who may or may not be robbing this orphanage he runs, but on the other hand the orphanage *is* taking care of orphans. So we have the doubts, and we have the cases we fuck up, and we have the cases we lose through no fault of our own. It never happens that way in crime fiction. Maybe that's why I read it – for escape from reality.'

McDonald, who knew O'Brien better than O'Brien realized, said, 'Something in particular is bugging you, Charles. Which case is it?'

O'Brien said, 'It's the goddam Weber thing. Remember last week I asked Tom Lynch to write to the District Attorney about his detective who's supposedly involved. Well, it had to be handled very delicately on Tom's level, because, as you know, Evelle Younger is making noises like he's going to run as the Republican candidate for Attorney General next year. Anyway, Tom wrote a beautiful letter, which you saw, asking that Younger's people give the detective a lie-detector test about his involvement in the Devins-Weber matter. Now *you* know that the polygraph isn't worth a shit, and *I* know it, and Evelle Younger knows it. But Younger uses it every day and pays a guy fifteen thousand dollars a year to run the machine in his office. He's been busting his ass, in fact, to get Devins to submit to the polygraph.

'But what happens when Tom asks him to put his man on the lie-detector? Just this morning Evelle writes back, refusing. He says, "I have a personal lack of confidence in the validity of the polygraph." As you know, we've been monitoring Weber's phone calls and the detective has been calling him from his home as much as four or five times a day. The minute we figure Tom's letter reached the DA's office, the phone calls to Weber stopped. How come things like this don't happen in the Simenon and J. J. Marric books?'

O'Brien still was grumbling when McDonald left his office about an hour later.

He grumbled all day.

Late in the afternoon Miles Rubin came in with the news that the Kirschke trial date had been set. It was August 14th, a little more than a month away.

O'Brien said, 'How do *you* feel about our case against Kirschke?'

'It's touch and go. I have my doubts.'

'So do I. That's one of the penalties of being halfway intelligent, I guess. The fool believes blindly, the intelligent man never ceases to doubt. I don't know who said that. Maybe *I* did.'

'You did,' commented Rubin dryly.

Pretending to ignore the Senior Assistant, O'Brien continued: 'I'd make a lousy politician, I guess. I'm like Adlai Stevenson. I always can see – maybe a little too clearly – the other fellow's point of view.'

'And you think there might be some validity to Kirschke's point of view?'

'Well,' said O'Brien, 'maybe he *did* leave the airport when he said he did. Maybe he *was* at Yermo too early to have committed the murders in Naples. We don't really have the evidence to disprove him completely. The problem is that Kirschke's been so obstreperous and obnoxious through this whole thing that maybe he colored our attitude and we wanted to nail him just for the sake of putting down a cocksure arrogant son of a bitch.'

'Are you losing your faith in the jury system, Charles?' said Rubin. 'They'll let us know if we're wrong.'

O'Brien muttered, 'I know. But you've got to be a mystic to believe in law enforcement.' He gestured toward a paper Rubin was holding in his hand. 'What else have you got for me?'

Rubin handed him a report on BNE narcotics agents who had been shot in recent operations. One agent had been wounded in the back by a man from whom he was trying to buy fifty kilos of marijuana. Another became involved in a running gun battle after making an undercover buy of just two ounces of heroin. The agent sustained a broken arm, a severed artery, and a bullet had lodged near his spine.

'There are too many guns pouring into this state,' roared O'Brien. 'It's getting to be like the goddam Wild West. Why can't we get our gun control laws through the goddam legislature?'

Rubin had heard this before and shrugged.

O'Brien looked at the report again and said, 'We've got a hundred good narcotics agents in the field and I don't want *any* of them to get hurt or killed. Brief me on what's going on in the BNE.'

'They've got two big operations scheduled. The first is called "Grab-bag." We're going to team up with all the local police departments and sweep every pusher we know about in Ventura County. The second is to try to nail Ramsaier and Verstraeten, the two guys who've been trading heroin for guns to sell to militants. Both of these characters always are armed and dangerous. Ramsaier has been shooting off his mouth about killing any agent or cop who even tries to question him.'

'When are these operations coming up?' O'Brien asked.

'Both of them tomorrow,' said Rubin glumly.

CHAPTER FOURTEEN

There was considerable tension behind the locked squad room doors of the Bureau of Narcotic Enforcement on the second floor of the Old State Building. It was only seven o'clock in the morning, but the BNE agents, arriving singly and in pairs from their homes, had been filtering in since about 5:30. The squad rooms looked strange, with twenty-four men clustered about sipping coffee and conversing quietly. Normally, about two-thirds of the agents are out in the field at any one given time, and the unusual assemblage of so many of them in their undercover clothing made the scene look like a prelude to a hippie protest demonstration.

At 7.20 A.M. field supervisor George Houston came in and dispatched his eight-man team to the basement arsenal to bring up the machine guns they were going to trade to Ramsaier and Verstraeten for heroin. A few minutes later the Houston team, led by Roger Livingston and Sixto Ramirez, staggered back into their squad room with the automatic weapons. There were German Schmeissers from World War II, spindly British Sten guns with folding stocks, and deadly but delicate-looking Israeli-made Uzis. All had been taken from the radical right-wing Minute Men in the C.I.I. raid of several months before, and each was capable of mowing down scores of people with its several-hundred-rounds-per-minute rate of fire.

The other agents gathered around and they examined the unfamiliar weapons with an almost childlike curiosity. Stan Friedman, one of the field supervisors, hefted an Israeli Uzi admiringly and sighted down the sleek barrel. 'The Nazi Schmeissers I can understand for the Minute Men,' he observed, 'but how could they compromise their anti-Semitic principles by using Jewish guns?'

At 7:45 A.M. Houston briefed his team. He told them that Russ Moeller, the Ventura Sheriff's undercover detective, had made contact with Ramsaier and would meet him sometime during the day to effect the trade of the guns for five ounces of heroin. 'Your job,' he said, 'is to cover Moeller and make the bust at the exact moment Squeak passes the smack. If the ass-hole pulls a gun, you've got to protect Moeller as well as yourselves. Blow the bastard up.' Instinctively Livingston removed his .38 from its holster under his loose-hanging green-and-purple sport shirt. He checked it to make sure it was clean. He asked, 'Where do we meet Moeller?'

'At the Regal Motel in Oxnard. I've booked a couple of rooms there and that'll be our headquarters. Another thing. The other two teams are scheduled to start Operation Grab-bag at ten o'clock tonight. We've *got* to rip Squeak and Unk before then. Otherwise, when pushers start getting busted all over the county, *our* two ass-holes will get scared and go to ground and we'll never catch up with them again.'

The eight-man Friedman team and the eight-man Cox team, named after the third field supervisor, listened glumly from the sidelines. Their job that day – Operation Grab-bag – was routine to them and, in a way, distasteful. These mass raids were scheduled from time to time and were considered to be wholly apart from their daily duty. The BNE men called such roundups 'PR capers' – PR standing for public relations. Since they had limited manpower and relied on the local sheriffs and police departments for extra men when needed, they, in turn, had to donate their expertise to the local sheriffs and police departments whenever the locals decided they required a rash of well-publicized wholesale arrests to impress the citizenry that they were on the ball in the narcotics area.

Ordinarily the BNE men did not prey on the dope-pushing small-fry or on children smoking pot in school, as the locals did. The state agents prided themselves in being an elite force, concentrating mainly on the major pushers operating across city and county lines. They even had an official set of minimums for themselves – five kilos of marijuana, ten jars of pills (a jar is a thousand tablets, usually barbiturates or amphetamines), or heroin in *any* amount. Tonight, for public relations purposes, they'd be arresting kids selling one-dollar rolls of five seconal capsules in parking lots. They were not enthusiastic about the impending night's work.

It was strictly a coincidence that the Squeak-Unk operation and Operation Grab-bag had come up on the same day. The ponderous machinery of Grab-bag, with hundreds of local narcotics officers involved along with a dozen disparate police forces, had been assembled over a two-week period. It now was too late to call it off or postpone it to another day. When the operation first had been planned, it was thought that Ramsaier and Verstraeten long since would have been trapped and arrested. Ramsaier, however, had been stalling Moeller for six days – on the grounds that he was having difficulty putting together so large a package as five ounces of heroin. It was only the night before that he had informed Moeller by phone that he now was ready to deal for the guns.

At 8 A.M. the Houston team moved out, two men per radio-equipped unmarked car. The guns were in the trunk of Livingston's Ford. While the others headed toward the Regal Motel headquarters in the city of Oxnard, on the Pacific Ocean north of Los Angeles, field supervisor Houston sped inland along the Ventura Freeway and then on Route 126 to the town of Santa Paula, where Verstraeten lived. Houston pulled up in front of the little Spanish-style police station just off the main street of the lovely agricultural community nestling in its own green valley. Dewey Dyer, the bulky middle-aged Deputy Chief of the Santa Paula Police Department, was waiting for him.

Houston shook hands with Dyer and glanced at the wall of the veteran cop's office which featured a forty-two-year-old class graduation photograph labeled 'Our Golden Memories.' Houston said, 'Are you all set for Grab-bag tonight?'

Dyer, scarcely able to contain his excitement, said, 'We sure are, George. Got eleven of my best men all primed to go.'

'Have you been keeping an eye on Verstraeten?'

'Sure have, George. He was in here the other night on the pretext of looking for a job. Said to let him know if we heard of anyone wanting a truck driver. But I could tell he was getting scared and worried. He said he wanted us to know there was a lot of narcotics around and he wondered – trying to pump us, of course – if it wasn't time for the state and federal men to be coming in here.'

'And what did you answer to that, Dewey?'

'I got properly indignant. I said we could handle all the narcotics problems that exist around here and we didn't need no help from the outside.'

Houston nodded. 'Did you know Verstraeten's a hype, Dewey?'

'You mean he shoots *smack?*'

'Yeah, one of our men saw him shooting in the kitchen of his house a few weeks ago. Tell me, Dewey, how did he get to teach kids weight lifting at the Boys' Club?'

Dyer said, 'Well, I never laid eyes on him until about a year ago when he came into town and showed up here at the police station to register as an ex-con. The next thing I knew he was working out with the weights at the Boys' Club – his arm is about the size of my head, you know – and then he was hired to be an instructor in weight lifting. When I found that out, I went to the president and vice-president of the Boys' Club. I'm a director of the club, see. I told the president and the vice-president Verstraeten was an ex-con with a three-page rap sheet, but they decided they should give him the benefit of the doubt because he was interested in helping youngsters. That's all I could do.'

'I see,' said Houston. 'Are Verstraeten's wife and baby here in town?'

'No, she left him and took the kid with her to some Southern state.'

'What about Ramsaier?'

'He's got a wife and *two* little kids, but I don't know where they are.'

'No, I mean how much do you know about *him?*'

'Well, he came here about eight, ten years ago, when he was in his teens. His mother is a nice respectable woman. A waitress. She always worked hard and gave him everything he wanted. The usual case. She was too damned busy providing what she *thought* were the important things. In the meantime the kid was always getting in trouble while she was away working at the restaurant. Nothing serious. He's too smart to get caught at the serious things.'

'What about now?' asked Houston.

'Well, he's got quite a reputation as a ladies' man. Also he's got quite a reputation for his temper. Plays a lot of pool.

One night he wasn't doing so well at the pool hall and he turned over the whole table. The man has the strength of an ox. That pool table must have weighed close to a half-ton.'

'But you never figured him for peddling smack or pot or anything?'

'No,' said Dyer ruefully.

'Tell me,' said Houston after a pause, 'do Ramsaier and Verstraeten hang out with anybody we maybe could twist to find out where they are, if we have to?'

'Well, there's all those hippie kids in Verstraeten's pad all the time. We get a lot of complaints from the neighbors about them. But I don't think you can work on them because they're all juveniles, fourteen to sixteen years old. Boys and girls both, they seem to flock to Verstraeten and Ramsaier. Consider them Marlon Brando-types or something. . . . But wait a minute, there *is* one kid, about eighteen, name of Jerry Kitchens. He's a wise guy, loudmouth, brags about taking all kinds of narcotics. From a good family, but a juvenile record for burglary. Was suspended from school. He might be a kind of runner for Ramsaier.'

'Do you have any idea where this kid Kitchens might be now?'

'Yes, as a matter of fact I do,' said Dyer, fumbling with papers on his desk. 'He's one of our targets for tonight in Grab-bag. One of my men saw him in the pool hall just around the corner about a half hour ago.'

Houston got up to go. 'Thanks, Dewey,' he said, 'and good hunting tonight.'

'Yeah,' said Dyer, smiling with anticipatory excitement, 'You, too.'

Houston left, drove around the block in his car and parked. He turned on the special-channel BNE radio which could not be heard by any other police force. He mentioned a code number into the microphone, repeated it, and then Livingston answered from his car in Oxnard, fifteen miles away. 'What's going on?' Houston asked.

Livingston said, 'Verstraeten's in his pad. Moeller just called him there. He said he didn't know where Squeak is but he expects to hear from him later. But *we* know where Squeak is. The Santa Barbara police just spotted him on the campus there. He's riding around in a classic red 1955 MG convertible, license number zebra love zebra two one nine. Quite a car for an ass-hole. I wish I had one.'

'It would be too small for your big head,' said Houston. 'Where's the red MG now?'

'We don't know. Santa Barbara lost it.'

'Okay, keep everybody on the alert for it. In the meantime I have a kid here, Jerry Kitchens, an ass-hole buddy of Ramsaier and Verstraeten in case we have to pick him up and twist him to find out where Ramsaier is.'

Livingston's metallic radio-voice said, 'Verstraeten's the one I'd like to twist. How about letting me pick him up and do it right now?'

Houston said grimly into the microphone, 'We don't twist anyone *yet*. Let's stick to the plan. Keep Moeller trying to make contact for the buy.'

'Okay, chief,' said Livingston.

'Wait for me at the motel,' said Houston. 'I'm coming in.'

When Houston arrived at the Regal Motel, set in a hamburger-stand-and-gasoline-station-studded strip on the outskirts of Oxnard, the two rooms he had chosen for a headquarters were a bedlam. Agents were sprawled all over the beds, a noxious shade of purple. Not only were his own men there, but people from the Cox team and the Friedman team also had drifted in. So had other men from various police forces and the Ventura County Sheriff's Department, all marking time while awaiting further orders for the start of Operation Grab-bag that night. There even were two young bearded Federal Narcotics Agents who had been assigned to Grab-bag to look around for matters of interest to the U.S. Attorney. Houston muttered to Livingston, 'Some security you have here. Any hype walking by would figure there's a narco agents' convention going on.'

Houston picked his way past a pinochle game in one corner and a poker game, for matchstick stakes, taking place on the floor of one of the rooms, and he beckoned to his two senior agents, Livingston and Ramirez, to follow him into the bathroom. As he closed the door of the john, Livingston chuckled and said, 'I'll never forget once when we were staying in this motel. Sixto was taking a shower and suddenly I saw him run out the door bare-ass naked except for his gun, which he picked up as he ran past the bed. While he was taking his shower he happened to look out the window and saw a guy making a smack buy in the parking lot. He made a good bust, too, with nothing but a towel covering his cock.'

'Forget about that now,' said Houston. 'What are all those guys doing here?'

'Shoemaker made this the command post for Operation Grab-bag, too,' said Ramirez. Houston fell silent. Shoemaker, the agent-in-charge for the Los Angeles area, was the boss of all of them. Houston said, 'Is Moeller here?'

Livingston said, 'Yeah, he's one of the guys playing poker. He's phoning Verstraeten every hour on the hour and Verstraeten keeps telling him he hasn't heard from Squeak yet but to be patient.'

'Any sign of the red MG?'

'It was seen outside the Pierpont Inn in Ventura. Then it took off again down Route 101. That guy really gets around.'

'Was he heading south?'

'That's what the Ventura police say, but they didn't follow him, like you said.'

'Then he might be heading our way. Have you briefed Moeller on what he's supposed to do?'

'Yes, but maybe while we've got some time we'd better go over it with him again. This is his first big case and we don't want him to blow.'

They pushed their way back into the noisy, smoky room and found Moeller who insisted on finishing a poker hand in which he was building a possible straight flush. He was an excitable young man, heavily moustached, but no more than twenty-three. While Houston waited for him to finish the hand, he observed the puppy-like activity going on in the room. Two agents were wrestling. Another was shouting, 'Now who's the wise son of a bitch who hid my gun and handcuffs I left here on the bed?' Everyone roared with laughter until the agent, a Deputy Sheriff, found the gun and handcuffs tucked away behind one of the lavender and yellow curtains.

Moeller lost the hand. The straight and the flush both were broken on the last card. He went out into the parking lot to talk. He listened intently and with respect. Livingston had guided his every move in the Ramsaier case, even telling him what to say in each of his telephone contacts, and his attitude toward Livingston was that of a freshman football rookie to an All-Pro quarterback He was even more deferential to Houston, whom he knew by reputation If Livingston was Joe Namath to Moeller, Houston was Weeb Eubank.

Livingston said, 'Like I told you, you're going to be in my car with the guns in the trunk and you're going to be all alone. Don't worry about us. We'll be close by When Ramsaier passes you the smack, go to the back of the car and raise the trunk lid to show him the guns. That'll be our signal – the raised trunk lid. We'll count five and then move in.'

'Yeah,' said Houston dryly, 'and if he starts shooting drop to the ground and roll under the car. If we have to blow him up, we don't want to hit you, too.'

Suddenly the jauntiness drained out of the face of the young Moeller.

They went back into the motel room. Ramirez joined the poker game, but one ear always was tuned to a portable BNE-channel radio he had placed on the bed beside him. Houston's other men were staked out down the street from Verstraeten's house and on the main highways, looking for the red MG. They kept reporting in regularly over the radio. The red MG was seen pulling up in front of Verstraeten's house in Santa Paula. It was there for five minutes and took off again, heading toward the mountain road to Ojai.

Moeller phoned Verstraeten. Unk said, 'Hey, man, Squeak was just here. He said to tell you he's tied up with a cunt this afternoon, but he'll meet you at the Ban-Dar Club at six o'clock. He's all set to deal.'

It then was 12:30 P.M., so there was nothing to do but wait for five and a half hours. Ramirez grumbled, 'This fuckin' job is just like the Army. We spend ninety per cent of our time waiting.' He rejoined the poker game, where he already had amassed a fortune in matchsticks.

At 1 P.M. the junior agents were sent out for sandwiches and coffee. Livingston told one of them, 'Get everybody to put their money up front or you guys are going to get burned.'

At 2 P.M. agent-in-charge Gerard Shoemaker came in and conferred briefly with Houston. Shoemaker mainly was worried about the timing. He told Houston, 'If you don't make your bust by ten o'clock, when Grab-bag is scheduled to start, we'll have to call you off.'

The food came and was consumed and the banter went on. Mostly it was about girls, but Houston, trying to concentrate on the special-channel radio, also heard some old snatches of conversation. One rough-looking agent said, 'My mother lives in Redwood City. I sent her ten dollars' worth of flowers for Mother's Day.' Someone kidded Sixto Ramirez about his nine children. 'Don't you chicanos ever read about the Pill? Or don't you read?' Ramirez did not deign to answer. He had heard this before and he knew there was a certain amount of envy in the remark. It was well-known that all his children were doing brilliantly in school and that his eldest, a junior college track star, was a fourteen-foot-nine-inch pole vaulter and one of the best in the country.

Houston half-listened to a discussion between Livingston and Shoemaker as to whether they would spend their week-end scuba diving, dune-buggying, or sailing. Houston said, 'These single guys. All they worry about is which toy to play with.' To himself he marveled, as he once had in World War II during the Battle of the Bulge, how men could converse so inconsequentially on what *could* be the eve of their impending deaths.

At 4 P.M. the radio crackled with the news that the red MG was parked outside the Capri Motel in Ojai. Houston went into the bathroom to talk with Livingston and Ramirez. He said, 'Let's go up to Ojai and stake this son of a bitch out so he can't slip away from us. We can follow him to the Ban-Dar Club for the six o'clock meet.'

Ramirez stayed behind with the radio to act as the control. Houston and Livingston took off in their cars for Ojai, a magnificent mountain resort community about twenty-five miles to the north and west. They sped along the scenic route, rising steadily from the coastal range, but when they got to the Capri Motel, the red MG was gone. Houston used his regular police radio to call the California Highway Patrol. Yes, they had seen the red MG. It had been spotted heading east to Santa Paula. 'Shit,' said Houston.

Houston and Livingston hastened back to Oxnard. It now was 5:30 and the scheduled meeting with Squeak at the Ban-Dar Club was only a half hour away. Livingston and Moeller hastily changed cars and the entire Houston team moved, by preplanned different routes, to take up their preplanned positions around the club. At six o'clock the only car visible was Moeller's, parked outside the club. There was no red MG.

At 6:30 Moeller went into the club to ask for Ramsaier. He hadn't been in all day.

By 7 P.M. neither the red MG nor Ramsaier had showed, so Houston, using the special-channel radio, ordered all his men to go back to the Regal Hotel. Houston waited for Moeller in the parking lot. 'Get your ass upstairs and try to reach Verstraeten on the phone,' he snarled.

It was 7:15. There was no answer at Verstraeten's house.

There was no answer, either, at 7:27, 7:46, 8:05, or 8:23.

Ramirez was philosophical about it. 'The trouble with dope pushers,' he observed, 'is that you never can count on them to keep appointments on time.'

'More likely,' Houston angrily said, 'some hype spotted this fuckin' convention here and warned off *everybody*.'

At 8:50 P.M. Houston dispatched John Fairburn, one of the trainee agents, to stake-out the Verstraeten house again and to inform them immediately if the red MG appeared.

At 9 P.M. agent-in-charge Shoemaker looked at his watch and said to Houston, 'You've got exactly one hour. What are you going to do?'

Houston said, 'Can't you put off this fuckin' Grab-bag until midnight? Our bust is worth more than all that nickel-and-dime stuff put together.'

They argued for a while and finally Shoemaker said, 'All right. I'll postpone until eleven o'clock. That gives you another hour. But I can't give you a minute more. At eleven sharp we have to move. It'll be too late to call off all the locals.'

Houston nodded and lapsed into a sullen silence. At 9:10 he said to Livingston, 'I guess we've blown it.'

At 9:11 the radio crackled. It was young John Fairburn's excited voice. 'The red MG's here,' he shouted. 'It's here – at Verstraeten's.'

Houston tore up the divided Highway 126 toward Santa Paula at ninety miles per hour. He couldn't see the other cars driven by Livingston, Ramirez, and Moeller, but he kept up a constant conversation with them on the radio. He slowed down when he reached the outskirts of Santa Paula and crept into South 4th Street with his headlights turned off. There was no red MG in front of Verstraeten's house. Just Moeller's car. It was 9:25 P.M. He tried to raise Fairburn on the radio to find out what had happened to the MG, but he got no answer.

At 9:32 Houston saw Moeller come out of the Verstraeten house, get into his car and drive off. Using the code number, Houston said into his radio microphone, 'All S units. Meet me in the parking lot of the Santa Paula police station.' When Houston reached the parking lot, Moeller and Livingston already were there. Moeller was almost dancing up and down with anticipation. He said to Houston, 'Ramsaier left word with Verstraeten for me to meet him outside the Loop's Restaurant in Ventura at 10:30.' Houston looked at his watch. It was 10:10, just fifty minutes to the start of Operation Grab-bag. 'Take off,' he said to Moeller.

Once again Houston sped down Route 126. He tried to count the number of times he had been on that particular stretch of road that day, but he was too weary. He arrived in Ventura at 10:31 and pulled into the parking lot of Loop's Restaurant. None of his men was there. Neither was the red MG. My God, he thought to himself, there's *another* Loop's Restaurant here in Ventura. He tried to put out a general call to all S units on his private-channel BNE radio. The radio was dead.

He rushed to the other Loop's, a few miles down Highway 101. No BNE cars. No red MG. It now was 10:40, twenty minutes to Grab-bag. Sweating profusely, Houston tried to re-order his thoughts to cope with the emergency. He suddenly remembered that Livingston was using Moeller's car and Moeller's car was equipped with a regular police-band radio. Houston kept switching channels as he called for any S unit to respond. Suddenly Livingston's voice came in loud and clear. He said, 'Moeller and Squeak have gone to the Carousel. It's a nightclub on a service road just down 101 from where you are.' It was 10:43.

At 10:45 Houston pulled up about fifty yards down the service road from the Carousel. Cacophonous rock music was blaring from the nightclub and patrons were bustling around the entrance. He could clearly see the red MG in the parking lot. Moeller's car was under a streetlamp in the otherwise dark road alongside the building. He could not see any of his other men.

At 10:47 Houston saw Moeller come out of the nightclub with an enormous blond youth in red-and-white striped bell-bottom pants and a baby-blue sport shirt. The music now had reached a crescendo with an almost unrecognizable version of 'Aquarius'. He watched Moeller and the youth push through the milling crowd at the entrance of the Carousel and wondered how many people would get hurt or killed if there was any shooting. He cursed to himself.

He saw the odd couple (Moeller is five feet eight to Ramsaier's six four) walk to Moeller's car. They conversed for a few seconds and then Houston saw Moeller go to the trunk of the car. He lifted the lid and Ramsaier peered inside. Houston counted to five. Nothing happened. Houston said to himself, 'My God, I'm going to have to make this bust myself – at my age.' He grabbed the loaded .38 beside his seat and sprinted from the car. Just then, however, he saw all his men materialize from nowhere out of the darkness. Livingston, Ramirez, Fairburn grabbed Ramsaier and flung him against the concrete wall of the building. Livingston twisted both huge arms behind the giant youth and snapped on the handcuffs. It was 10:54.

In the few seconds it took Houston to reach the scene, Ramsaier had been pushed back into the darkness beyond the street-light. The music still was blaring and the crowds in front of the Carousel had no idea of what had taken place just a few feet away.

Ramsaier was standing disconsolately, his hands behind his back, when Houston walked up to him. Houston noted how much he looked like the old movie actor, Sonny Tufts. Moeller, having participated in his first big arrest, was once again dancing with excitement. Livingston and Ramirez were their usual phlegmatic selves. 'He took a cool bust,' Livingston said. 'He didn't want to get shot.'

'Did he have a gun?' Houston asked.

'Yes,' said Livingston, 'a .45. But he left it inside with the bartender.'

'Then you think maybe he suspected this might be a bust.'

'Maybe.'

'Then why did he go through with it?'

'Greed. Those guns would have brought him thirty, forty thousand dollars from the militants. Besides, he probably wasn't really *sure* he was being set up.'

Ramsaier, still partly in shock, was pleading for a cigarette. Houston lit one and put it between his lips. He asked the prisoner, 'Were you thinking of shooting it out?'

Ramsaier said, 'If you were locals, yes. But I knew you'd blow my ass off.'

A Ventura Sheriff's patrol car glided up silently with its lights off. Ramsaier was taken off to the Ventura County jail to be booked.

Houston and Livingston examined the red MG. They found a packet of marijuana in the glove compartment. Under the front seat were twenty rounds of .45 caliber ammunition. On the seat was a picture of Ramsaier's wife and two beautiful blond babies, and fifteen books of meticulously mounted Triple-S Blue Stamps.

As Houston drove away, the music from the Carousel was 'I Get a Little Help from My Friends.'

Operation Grab-bag got under way at 11 P.M., exactly six minutes after the Ramsaier arrest. Livingston was in on the Verstraeten arrest – by his own request – a half hour later. He and six other agents burst through the door of Verstraeten's house and found him on the couch, watching TV and fondling a fifteen-year-old girl. Verstraeten reached under the pillows of the couch for a .22 automatic, but Livingston jumped on his arm with both feet and broke his wrist.

Jerry Kitchens was picked up outside his home as he sold ten dollars' worth of heroin to an undercover Sheriff's Deputy. Kitchens' mother was looking on as the arrest was made. She wept bitterly and said, 'I had an idea he was fooling around with marijuana, but *heroin*, God help us!'

In all, seventy-five people were arrested in Operation Grab-bag.

CHAPTER FIFTEEN

It was two days before O'Brien received the complete reports on the Ramsaier-Verstraeten case and Operation Grab-bag, though Miles Rubin had briefed him sketchily the morning after the all-night raids. O'Brien expressed grumpy gratification to Rubin that no one, including Ramsaier or any of his agents, had had 'his ass blown off.' He was touchy on the subject, not only because of concern for his men, but because an unfortunate incident had taken place a few weeks before. Two BNE agents had been out drinking with some local narco officers just prior to a raid. During the raid one of the locals had fired his gun through the floor of the suspect's apartment and had killed an innocent neighbor in the apartment downstairs. O'Brien had insisted that the cop be prosecuted and he had suspended his own two men.

O'Brien, after reading the complete Ramsaier reports, summoned Rubin and said, 'This case smells like a lot more than just an isolated bust. In fact, it smells like an organized crime deal to me. Did Livingston interrogate Ramsaier?'

Rubin said, 'Yes. He got to him in the Ventura County jail just before some high-priced lawyer sprang him on bail. Ramsaier was afraid to talk. He told Roger he was more scared of the people he worked for than he was of us.'

O'Brien sucked thoughtfully on his pipe, causing Rubin to duck ostentatiously away from the billowing acrid smoke. The Chief Deputy ignored him. He said, 'The people he worked for, eh? Did Roger get any other leads out of him?'

'Yes. When Ramsaier wouldn't talk, our boy wonder gave him the sympathetic bit, asking him how such a nice clean-cut young fellow could get himself in such a terrible mess, and all that crap.'

'And?'

'Ramsaier finally broke down and told him he was a heavy gambler and that he had dropped a load in Las Vegas. It was someone there who told him about the gun deal and how he could make a lot of money fast to pay off his Vegas debts.

Not that he hadn't been dealing in dope before. But this, I suspect, is what kicked him up into the big time.'

'Does Roger have any idea how to go about finding out who Ramsaier's suppliers were?'

'The boy wonder is one step ahead of you. He checked all his informants yesterday and he's come up with some good leads. There's one guy, a legitimate businessman on the surface, who owns a couple of bars, a used car lot, and whatnot. He also has a couple of private planes, which fly back and forth to Mexico and every once in a while into Santa Barbara and Oakland. Roger thinks this guy might have been selling the smack to Ramsaier and then buying the guns from him for resale to the militants. He's got a bodyguard, a big tough son of a bitch who the informant says is his enforcer. He enforces with an Army Browning automatic rifle.'

'I know the weapon well,' said O'Brien. 'It's enough to scare the shit out of anybody. Did Roger's songbirds tell him about anyone else?'

'Yes, and this one will really throw you. There's a doctor, a genuine M.D., seems to have been Ramsaier's supplier for pep pills and bennies. Roger checked up on this guy and found he's been ordering three and a half million amphetamine capsules every six months from pharmaceutical houses back East. Says they're for weight control of patients, but he'd have to have ten thousand very fat patients to use up that much. The informant tells Roger the doctor arranges to have his car robbed every once in a while to protect himself from the Feds.'

O'Brien sighed. 'So we seem to have uncovered just one corner of a giant web' he said. 'Make sure Roger stays on it, and better tip off the Feds, too. This one probably is interstate, too big for us to handle alone.'

Rubin, already burdened with a hundred other matters, nodded wearily. 'These cases *do* go on and on,' he said.

But many of the cases in the Old State Building do *not* go on and on. While O'Brien and Rubin were conversing, Andrea Ordin, one floor above them, was gloomily contemplating the fact that she faced defeat in the art frauds case – at least the Los Angeles segment of it with which she had been entrusted. She stared unseeingly at the vase of huge, gay paper flowers that had been placed on her windowsill to brighten her dark moments. The flowers did not relieve her black mood.

Andrea was not used to losing. Her life had been a series of small triumphs over the disadvantages of her attractiveness and her femininity in a man's world. She had used her attractiveness to *advantage* when she had worked her way through UCLA by getting jobs as an actress in small regional theater companies and on TV. To pay her way in the UCLA law school, she had worked part-time as a legal secretary and full-time as an editorial assistant in the Los Angeles bureau of *Newsweek*.

Because of her involvement in social causes, she had turned down lucrative private-practice offers when she graduated from law school, and she went to work immediately with the Attorney General's office. She was one of only three women lawyers in the AG's Los Angeles office (the other two were black) and operating in concert with them, and individually, she had compiled an imposing record of success in constitutional rights and consumer fraud cases. Her personal life had been a success, too. She had fought off the advances of every handsome young attorney in the office and had waited out the divorce of her husband, attorney Robert Ordin, until they were able to get married. And then, in her most significant triumph of all, she had won over the affections of Ordin's two teen-age children.

But now Andrea was about to lose.

She decided, however, to review the investigative reports once more before she reported her failure to O'Brien. Perhaps there was something she had overlooked.

The reports consisted of hundreds of pages, mostly prepared for her by Leroy Sana after he had completed his electronic wizardry in the Devins-Weber case. He had gone out into the field and had interviewed dozens of art fraud perpetrators and victims. None of the victims would file complaints or testify in criminal actions. Some of them openly expressed their fear to Sana that if they did become involved in cases for the State, they would expose themselves to possible prosecution by the Federal Government for income tax fraud.

As Sana unraveled the principal skein of the defalcations, a typical fraud would proceed like this:

Art Dealer A would approach Rich Man B, offering to sell him a Rouault for five thousand dollars. 'Now mind you,' the art dealer would say, 'this Rouault, while a very good example of the work of the master, is not authenticated. However, I know Art Expert C, who will write a verification of the painting as a genuine Rouault and give it an evaluation of forty thousand dollars. I also know Small College D, which will accept the Rouault as a donation worth Art Expert C's estimate of forty thousand dollars. Therefore, if you pay me, Art Dealer A, my price of five thousand dollars, you then can donate it to Small College D and take a forty thousand dollar deduction on your Federal income tax return. You thus make thousands of dollars on the deal, in that you will save that much on your income tax.'

Sana uncovered many such cases. 'The problem is,' he wrote in his report, 'when the Attorney General comes to Rich Man B and tells him his Rouault is a fake, does Rich Man B welcome him with open arms? In general he will tell us we are outrageous people even to ask him to testify. Small College D also is outraged. It would rather keep a fake on display than risk a scandal that could affect its other endowments.'

While such cases emerged as the classics, Sana found other versions of the fake-painting ploy. So-called art masterpieces were being given to banks as security for loans sometimes reaching into the hundreds of thousands of dollars. As Sana wrote, 'Bankers know nothing about art. They rely solely on the *provenance*, which could be a written authentication by someone like Art Expert C, who will verify anything for twenty dollars – plus a written history of the work, also thoughtfully provided by Art Expert C.' The same is true, Sana discovered, of insurance company investigators looking into allegedly valuable art works lost in contrived fires and house burglaries. Sana reported that at least he was able to convince bankers and insurance companies that in the future they should rely on the true, dispassionate, learned experts for evaluations of paintings.

After considerable frustration, Sana decided to concentrate on a single painting and one group of people, in order to make an example case that would put the entire machinery out of business. The painting was an alleged Rembrandt, *Rabbi with a Turban*, which to his knowledge never had been authenticated by a 'true, dispassionate, learned expert.' The people involved were Rich Man B (in this instance a wealthy and powerful politician); Art Dealer A (a so-called bedroom collector who operated out of his home); Art Expert C (an eighty-year-old former museum director who sold his 'authentications' for twenty-five dollars or less); a frightened semi-honest gallery owner; and the Hungarian refugee art restorer, Istvan Kovacs.

Sana first picked up the trail with the semi-honest gallery owner, who nearly fainted when the C.I.I. agent flashed his credentials. He informed Sana he had first seen *Rabbi with a Turban* in the gallery of a man who told him the work was an old painting but not an old master and could be described without misrepresentation only as 'of the *school* of Rembrandt.' The man said he had sold the work to Art Dealer A, the bedroom collector, for six thousand dollars.

The next time the semi-honest gallery owner had seen *Rabbi with a Turban* was in the home of Art Dealer A. The portrait now had a valuation of $1,800,000 and had been verified as an authentic Rembrandt by Art Expert C.

Sana went to see Art Expert C. The old man was doddering but alert. Sana asked him about his qualifications. He said he had helped found an art museum in 1930 but had left the organization a year or two later.

'That was nearly forty years ago,' said Sana. 'What have you been doing since?'

'I've been involved in various aspects of the art business,' said the expert.

'Was that your sole source of income?' asked Sana.

'No,' said the expert. 'Until 1957 I worked in aircraft plants in the Los Angeles area.'

Sana pulled out of his briefcase two authentications and appraisals of *Rabbi with a Turban* written by Art Expert C. One was dated September 15, 1966, and valued the painting at $750,000. The other was dated December 9, 1966, and stated, 'I place its value conservatively at $1,800,000.' Both *provenances* were written in florid prose, such as:

This painting accords with all the known grandeur and style of Rembrandt Van Rijn (1606–1669), the great Dutch Master of the 17th Century, from whose hand have come the greatest works of man's creativity in the fine arts. This work presented belongs to the year 1642 in the middle of his great second period when he was performing many similar portraits of the refugees who had found their way from eastern Europe to Amsterdam, where the artist befriended many and employed them as models for his compositions.

Sana asked, 'How come the value went up more than a million dollars in less than four months?'

The elderly Art Expert shrugged. 'It's a matter of judgment,' he said.

Sana said, 'You mention in the authentications that the work previously had been verified by Dr. W. Suida, a great art historian in New York. Do you know Dr. Suida?'

'I never met him, but I think he was an art dealer in New York.'

'Not a great art historian?'

'No, a dealer.'

Sana changed the subject. 'Where did you physically examine *Rabbi with a Turban* to make your authentications?'

'In the home of Istvan Kovacs. He had ten paintings in all, which he wanted me to verify.'

'Did you verify them all as authentic?'

'Of course. I've never known Mr. Kovacs to have a fake in his collection.'

'How much did Mr. Kovacs pay you for the ten *provenances?*'

'Two hundred and fifty dollars.'

Sana left and went to the home of Istvan Kovacs, the art restorer. Kovacs wasn't there, but the agent spoke to his wife. 'Istvan hasn't had a paintbrush in his hand since he left Hungary,' she volunteered in the course of the conversation. *Rabbi with a Turban* was hanging on the wall directly over her head.

Since *Rabbi with a Turban* was supposed to be in the possession of Art Dealer A, the bedroom collector, Sana decided to pay him a visit in his home, a few miles away in the San Fernando Valley. As the bedroom collector opened the door, the first thing Sana saw was *Rabbi with a Turban* hanging on *his* living-room wall.

Sana asked, 'What do you claim your *Rabbi* is worth?'

The bedroom collector said, 'A million eight hundred thousand.'

'I see,' said Sana, looking around the shabby home. 'And would you mind if the criminologists in our laboratory examine it?'

'Not at all,' said the dealer, beaming. 'What techniques would they use?'

'The neutron activated analysis method. It identifies the age of the pigments electronically.'

The dealer paled visibly. 'Oh, no,' he said. 'I've heard that boils the paints and ruins the painting.' Originally jovial, he terminated the interview as quickly as possible, saying he had to go to the hospital.

The next day Sana went back to see the semi-honest gallery owner who had started him on the trail of the Rembrandt *Rabbi*. Sana asked him about the two identical paintings he had seen. The gallery owner said, 'It's funny you should bring that up. There's a rich man, a big politician, who came in here and looked at my paintings and got very upset, and he asked me almost the exact same question. He said, "Is it possible that the same painter would ever paint the identical picture more than once?" When I told him no he got very angry and said he had bought some old masters that were brush-by-brush the same as some I had hanging in my gallery.'

Sana asked if the Rich Man had mentioned the name of the dealer who had sold him the identicals. The gallery owner said yes.

It was Art Dealer A.

Sana asked the gallery owner if Art Dealer A ever used the services of an art restorer. The gallery owner said, 'Yes, and strangely enough, the rich man also does business with the same fellow to retouch and varnish his paintings. He's a Hungarian, name of Istvan Kovacs.'

Sana returned to the San Fernando Valley to see Kovacs. This time he was at home. The art restorer was extremely nervous. Sana began slowly, asking him about his background. Kovacs said he had fled Hungary during the 1956 revolution and had come to the United States to work as a janitor in Pittsburgh. He then had moved to New Jersey where, because he had been 'an accomplished artist in Hungary,' he had opened an art studio where he did restoration work on old paintings. Some Hungarian friends had told him about their success 'in your wonderful state of California,' so he moved to Los Angeles and got a hundred-dollar-a-week job doing repair work on frames and canvases for one of the La Cienega Boulevard art galleries. Kovacs said he wheeled and dealed in paintings and eventually had enough money to open his own studio in the San Fernando Valley. It was then that he got to know Art Dealer A and others of his ilk. He also was introduced to Rich Man B and for a period of several months he actually was on the wealthy politician's payroll, at a salary of $800 per month, restoring paintings in the man's sizable collection.

Gradually Sana worked up to the key questions. He asked, 'Can you explain how this man came into possession of what he thought were original old masters that were identical with paintings hanging in a gallery?'

Kovacs was outraged. He said, 'Are you implying that I made *copies* of the paintings?'

Sana said, 'As a matter of fact, I am.'

Kovacs' wife said, 'But I told you Istvan hasn't had a paint-brush in his hand to make a painting ever since he left Hungary.'

'Nevertheless,' said Sana, 'I'd like to know how two sets of the same paintings came into existence, presumably after one set was left with you by a dealer.'

Kovacs finally broke down and admitted he had made copies of the originals for the rich man, 'who was interested in some decorative paintings for his office.' He had no idea, he said, that the rich man actually had shown them in his collection as genuine works of art.

'Now,' said Sana, 'how about the Rembrandt, *Rabbi with a Turban?* Was that one of the paintings you copied?'

Kovacs by now was terrified. 'Yes,' he mumbled.

'Was that why I saw one here and one in the dealer's house?'

'Yes,' said Kovacs.

'Did you paint the original, too, the one that's supposed to be worth a million eight hundred thousand dollars?'

Kovacs was nearly weeping. 'No, no,' he said.

'Which *is* the original – yours or the dealer's?'

'The dealer's. It's a real Rembrandt. I copied it for my own enjoyment when the dealer sent it here for the appraiser to verify.'

'Was *Rabbi with a Turban* one of the paintings the dealer sold to your rich man friend and which he returned when he found out there were duplicates around?'

'I don't know. I swear I don't know. All I can tell you is that the painting is hanging in the dealer's house right now.'

'And maybe here, too,' said Sana, looking at the blank space on the wall where the *Rabbi* had been displayed when he had been there a few days before.

At that point Sana thought he had a case – that in the rich man he had found a victim who would be willing to testify. He left the shattered Kovacs and spent a week trying to contact the wealthy politician at his home or office. The rich man never was in. He finally sent word to Sana that he did not wish to see him under any circumstances.

In his final report Sana wrote:

> Kovacs' position leaves a lot to be desired, but without a victim we have no case. The victim alone would be able to tie all the allegations together, but he refuses to co-operate. This may be because he has one of the best-known collections in California and has obtained sizable income-tax deductions through donations of parts of his collection to various universities and museums. In the absence of the victim's cooperation, reporting agent believes the information presented in this investigation does not support a prosecution for fraud.

Andrea Ordin studied this paragraph intently for a few minutes. She looked over the notes she had taken during her review of Sana's findings, and there was nothing she hadn't considered in a dozen previous reviews. She shrugged, straightened out her panty-hose, put on fresh lipstick, and steeled herself for a confrontation with O'Brien.

Even in more pleasant circumstances O'Brien always was a

little gruff with her. This, he had explained, was because he felt that if women's liberationists wanted to compete with men and earn the same salaries, they had to accept the fact of being *treated* like men. He was gruff with his male attorneys, too.

But now, as she outlined Sana's reports and told her story to O'Brien, the Chief Deputy was unexpectedly gentle.

'All right,' he said when she had finished her presentation, 'at least we've scared these bastards enough so that they'll probably go into some other line of work. Maybe you'll catch them passing fake diamonds to each other.'

'But I don't like losing,' said Andrea.

'Only Perry Mason wins 'em all,' said O'Brien.

Just down the hall in his Kirschke case command post, Albert Harris's pragmatic mind was not imaginative enough to dwell on Perry Mason's fictional invincibility, but similar envious thoughts crossed his mind. He looked around the room, now literally bulging with accordion files, and he wondered how he was going to pull together all the loose ends before the beginning of the trial on August 14th. He intimately knew the holes in his case and he had been unable to plug them to his satisfaction – despite the constant stream of witnesses and potential witnesses brought to the office for interviews by the C.I.I. agents since the Grand Jury hearings in June. Like Andrea Ordin he did not relish the idea of losing. He was sourly contemplating the possibility when he heard the door of his office open. He didn't even look up. He thought it was Robert Samoian with more bad news about surprise defense witnesses which the press predicted almost daily after chats with Kirschke's lawyer, the Silver Fox.

But a completely different voice said, 'Hi.'

Harris raised his tired, bloodshot eyes and saw Gene Frice. The agent still was in his army major's uniform, his green beret perched stolidly on his blondish head. Frice was limping slightly.

'Well, well, well,' said Harris, 'the soldier boy is back from his games. How was the vacation?'

Frice, accustomed to Harris after the pre-Grand Jury investigation, grinned. 'Oh, it was a lot of fun,' he said.

'Parachuting into the middle of Alaska, spraining my ankle in that nice half-frozen tundra, wet all the time, mosquitoes as big as your fist, trying to teach guerrilla tactics to a bunch of Indians and Eskimos who are only interested in suing the Federal Government for appropriation of their lands. Yes, sir, I tell you, it was a ball.'

Harris managed a smile. 'Anyway,' he said, 'I see you're wearing the wrong overalls. Are you ready to go back to work?'

'Tomorrow morning,' said Frice.

'Which phase of this tatterdemalion case do you want to work on?'

'Kirschke's gun,' said Frice grimly.

CHAPTER SIXTEEN

The Kirschke murder case began, as scheduled and advertised, on August 14th. However, unlike fictional courtroom drama on the screen and the printed page, it began with a whisper rather than a shout. The judge, Kathleen Parker, already had announced that she would devote herself to hearing pre-trial motions, so the courtroom, except for counsel and a handful of the press, was nearly deserted. The public preferred to wait to attend the trial after the dry stuff had been dispensed with and the juicier evidence began.

As in all real-life trials, the 'dry stuff' consumed a lot of time – here, more than a week. If it happened this way on television, Perry Mason and all the other lawyer-series never would have survived the first Nielsen rating. Yet everything that was to occur later in *The People* vs. *Kirschke* hinged on the droning arguments of the lawyers in those first few days of 'dry stuff.'

The courtroom, Department 108, was indistinguishable from the dozens of others in the forbidding Hall of Justice, whose Victorian sternness was accented by the contrast of the glistening new glass-and-marble Music Center to the west and even by the granite and steel Old State Building to the south. The actual room where Kirschke's fate would be decided was comparatively small and paneled in dark wood. As you entered, there were a few benches for spectators, then a wooden railing, beyond which both defense counsel and the prosecutors sat at a long table, one group to the left and the other to the right. Facing them from the bench was Judge Parker, a slim, graying, fifty-two-year-old woman, a discreet strand of nine-millimeter pearls peeking over the collar of her somber judicial robes. There was a witness stand to her left; a clerk, a court stenographer, and a bailiff to her right; an empty jury box – and that was all. One of the few spectators was Kirschke's twenty-two-year-old son, Doug, a gangling youth with some of his father's country-boy mannerisms. The judge had granted him the right to act as a 'runner' for the defense, but he mostly sat with his head in his hands.

In the absence of hard news those first few days, the press concentrated on writing profiles of the principal protagonists in the upcoming legal drama. Defense counsel Albert C. S. Ramsey, the Silver Fox, drew most of the attention. Mary Neiswender of the Long Beach *Press-Telegram* described him as 'wily and colorful,' and quoted 'contemporaries' as saying, 'He's an attorney who tries a case by the seat of his pants – and he's always out for the jugular vein. He'll chew up that prosecution and spit them out before they know what's happened.'

Miss Neiswender traced the career of the fifty-four-year-old Silver Fox from the time he was a Canadian farm boy until he worked his way through the University of Southern California Law School and became one of Long Beach's best-known attorneys. She wrote:

> 'In court you're a prizefighter,' the fifty-four-year-old court-room veteran says. 'You don't fight in the back alley or brawl in a bar. When the bell rings you fight, and in a fight you go out to win. I always wanted to be a fighter. They're brave people.'
>
> Ramsey is a pro. Considered one of the – if not THE – best criminal attorneys in the state, his courtroom fights have become legend.

Miss Neiswender wrote with equally gushing prose about Judge Parker, who, she revealed, was born in Minnesota, took her law degree at Pacific Coast University, and was brilliant in private practice until she was appointed to a municipal court judgeship in 1957 and eventually ascended, through the California election process, to the Superior Court.

Miss Neiswender wrote of Judge Parker:

> Contrary to what some attorneys may think when she smiles down at them from the bench, she's all judge. The first woman ever elected to a Superior Court of Los Angeles County without first having been appointed by the Governor, she defeated fourteen male candidates in the primary to do it.

So two more attorneys – even though they're the best – don't fluster her.

Concerning Kirschke, the reporters concentrated on his long-suffering stoicism-laced-with-humor. Again, Miss Neiswender, the local Dorothy Kilgallen of this trial:

> Meanwhile, Jack Kirschke sits on his side of the counsel table, conferring with his attorney, chatting with press representatives, waving to friends and planning his future. 'My son Doug is planning to buy a sailboat when he gets out of the Marine Corps, and we plan to sail around the world. Of course, that girl he brought to court today isn't in our plans. But they sure make a nice-looking couple.'

Concerning Harris, the most colorful thing Miss Neiswender or any of the other reporters could find to say was, 'He's an attorney's attorney.' They did not even mention Samoian.

Yet, as the pre-trial arguments droned on, the press began to realize that the two Attorney General's Deputies were winning considerably more points than they were losing. It somehow didn't fit the script. Ramsey paced up and down, his white mane flowing, as he gesticulated with dramatic emphasis, using his heavy black-framed eyeglasses in his hand as a pointer. Harris just sat behind his table, rarely getting to his feet, never raising his voice. Ramsey was particularly effective after the second day of pre-trial, when word got around that nude photos of the dead Elaine Kirschke would be shown in court, and the spectators' seats filled up, with a waiting line outside. But at the end of the day, after Ramsey had lost two motions, one of the reporters wrote, 'Ramsey apparently was able to convince the gallery, but not the judge.' The box score to date was:

Ramsey attempted to get the trial shifted to Long Beach, his home turf. He lost.

Ramsey made a motion to exclude any evidence concerning what Elaine Kirschke had told the Jolly Girls. He lost –

Ramsey tried to exclude testimony from neighbors who had heard the Kirschkes arguing. He lost.

Ramsey tried to exclude testimony about the time it took C.I.I. agent Allen to drive a car similar to Kirschke's from Naples to Yermo. He lost.

Ramsey tried to exclude the evidence of Kirschke's blood-flecked sport shirt and the we-will-sleep-alone-and-not-cohabit note written by Elaine. He won, as Harris had expected, on Constitutional grounds of illegal search-and-seizure.

But more important than all of these issues combined, there were two other Constitutional matters on which Harris knew the entire case hinged in these undramatic pre-trial maneuvers. If Ramsey won, there would *be* no case.

The first was the circumstances leading to Kirschke's arrest in Victorville the Monday morning after the murders. Ramsey argued that the arrest was illegal and therefore all of Kirschke's statements to the police and all investigative action based on them were inadmissible as 'the fruit of a poisoned tree.' The Silver Fox put six police officers on the stand and proved there was no legal justification for issuing an all-points bulletin for Kirschke's arrest that Monday morning. Ramsey won, and the Attorney General's case seemed to have gone down the drain. Particularly, the all-important evidence about the murder weapon, the .38 caliber Harrington and Richards Defender, would have to be excluded because Kirschke, after his arrest, told one of the police officers he had owned such a gun.

On the sixth day of pre-trial hearings Harris reopened the matter with Judge Parker. He lost again. On the seventh day Harris once again brought up the 'fruit of the poisoned tree' ruling. He cited previous cases he had researched all night, to prove that the tree was *not* poisoned – that Kirschke, as an experienced law enforcement official, knew his rights better than anyone and could have refrained from saying anything. This time Harris won. Judge Parker reversed her previous ruling.

The second crucial Constitutional question involved Ramsey's contention that Kirschke could not be given a fair trial because of the inordinate amount of pre-trial publicity about the case. The Silver Fox cited the United States Supreme Court decision which reversed the conviction of Dr. Sam Sheppard because of the unrestrained press coverage prior to *his* trial for the murder of *his* wife. Harris expected this motion and was prepared for it.

Gesturing toward Ramsey, Harris quietly told the judge: 'It's true – there has been a deluge of publicity. But ninety-five per cent of it has come from Mr. Kirschke himself, or from Mr. Ramsey, his attorney. My own office has maintained a policy of not issuing statements about the case.

'Previously the defense – which now cites unfavorable publicity as sufficient to prevent selection of a proper jury – was denied a motion to remove these proceedings to Long Beach on the grounds that it should be heard in the community where the crime was perpetrated. It is a fact that there has been more publicity about this case in Long Beach than in any other community in the country.

'I believe the defense has been working to achieve the best of all possible worlds, *providing* publicity to create a favorable public image which could lead prospective jurors to favor an acquittal, while using this motion as grounds for an appeal if there is a conviction.'

Judge Parker was convinced. Harris won. The trial was ordered to begin with the selection of a jury the next day, August 25th. The 'dry stuff' of the pre-trial procedure had taken nine court days.

But Ramsey had yet another maneuver to employ. He arrived in the courtroom the following morning with a worn brown Bible under his arm and made a motion to the judge that would eliminate any mention of the death penalty in selecting the jury. The Silver Fox's voice broke, his eyes filled with tears, and clutching his Bible, he flippped it open to Matthew, Luke, Romans, and Hebrews 10, quoting such passages as 'Vengeance is mine . . . saith the Lord.' He thrust his handkerchief into his mouth, choking back a sob, and said, 'I say to this court that a great majority of sincere Christian people, and certainly a majority of Christians who believe in God Almighty, will not sit on a jury where they must vote the death penalty. . . . Most people feel life itself is from God Almighty and death can only be decreed by Him. . . . The prosecutor is merely trying to fill the jury box with twelve hard-nosed people who will say, "I'll kill. . . ." '

Samoian looked at Harris and muttered, 'Oh, brother.'

Harris pulled himself to his feet and said, 'Your Honor, I

have seen on these old TV movies the headlines, "DA Demands Death Penalty." Maybe Mr. Ramsey has something like that in mind. I don't have any intention of saying anything of the kind here, now or later.'

The judge denied the Silver Fox's motion. She ordered the first prospective jurors to be brought into the courtroom.

It was a dramatic moment.

Twelve people in various degrees of bewilderment filed in from the room next door and seated themselves uncertainly in the jury box. Judge Parker then began the time-worn ritual, which, no matter how many times they had heard it, still brought a flutter of excitement to everyone in the room.

The judge said, 'The People against Jack Kirschke.'

Harris said, 'Ready for the People.'

Ramsey said, 'The defendant is present, Your Honor.'

The clerk read off the names of the twelve prospective jurors, spelling each in turn after they had been sworn in.

Then, continuing the ritual, the following took place:

JUDGE PARKER: Ladies and gentlemen, the defendant in this case, Jack Kirschke, has been charged by indictment with two felonies. In Count One, it is alleged that on or about the 8th day of April, in the County of Los Angeles, the said defendant did willfully, unlawfully, and feloniously, and with malice aforethought murder Elaine Terry Kirschke, a human being. This is in violation of Section 187 of the Penal Code of California, commonly referred to as murder.

The judge repeated the same charges for Count Two, the murder of Drankhan. Then:

JUDGE PARKER: The defendant has previously been arraigned on the charge contained in the indictment, he has entered his plea of not guilty, and he stands here now for trial. Mr. Kirschke, would you rise for a moment, please, and face the jury?

(Mr. Kirschke arises and faces the jury.)

JUDGE PARKER: Thank you. You may be seated. Mr. Kirschke is represented by his counsel, Mr. Ramsey.

(Mr. Ramsey stands and faces the jury.)

JUDGE PARKER: The People are represented by the Assistant Attorney General, Mr. Harris.

(Mr. Harris stands and faces the jury.)

JUDGE PARKER: And the Deputy Attorney is Mr. Samoian.

(Mr. Samoian stands and faces the jury.)

JUDGE PARKER: I shall ask you a few questions collectively. It is anticipated that this case will take some time to try. It will probably go four to six weeks and it could go longer. Is there anyone to whom it would be a hardship if they were impaneled on a jury in this case and the case would go that long?

One of the prospective jurors, Mrs. Helen Palmer, stood up. She pleaded hardship and was excused. Harris watched her go, and he knew that with all the jurors who would be excused by the judge, and with all the questions he and Ramsey would ask dozens of others, and with the twenty challenges each, which he and Ramsey could use to eliminate people unacceptable to them, it would take at least two weeks before a jury finally would be impaneled.

Harris suddenly realized he had a splitting headache.

CHAPTER SEVENTEEN

One morning later that week, O'Brien, too, had a splitting headache. It was not, however, because of worry over the Kirschke case. He traced his indisposition to an excellent bottle of 1967 Château Lascombes he had enjoyed with Tom MacDonald at dinner the night before at the Windsor Restaurant. O'Brien decided the wine had been insufficiently aged, in which event he knew from experience he could quench the headache with a liberal dosage of aspirin. He did so. Then, because the Lo-Tel Motel already was stirring with the sounds of bedsprings and wheel-borne salesmen's sample cases, he decided to go to his office, though it was only 7:30.

When O'Brien arrived, he noticed a light through the frosted glass of Lynch's office, which the Attorney General hadn't used since Harris had appropriated it as his command post. The Chief Deputy went in and found Harris hunched over an accordion file like a crow over carrion. Harris's eyes were red, and his iron-gray wiry hair was in disarray, standing up in little pickets all over his head.

'You look terrible,' O'Brien said. 'You were thirty-seven years old when you started this case. How old are you now?'

Harris said, 'A *hundred* and thirty-seven. It's all this luxurious living in the Biltmore and the Hilton down here. Maybe I should move into the Lo-Tel Motel.'

O'Brien grinned. 'You can get just as tired from not sleeping in the Lo-Tel as from not sleeping in the Hilton.' He noticed a list of names on Harris's desk. 'How's the jury selection going?' he asked.

'Slowly,' said Harris. 'The Silver Fox even asks them what television news shows they watch and the names of their favorite TV commentators.'

'And how about you?'

'Oh, I'm being equally intransigent. I've used up five challenges so far and Ramsey has used six. We've only seated two jurors.'

'I can't wait to drop into the courtroom some day to hear

your jam-jar explanation of circumstantial evidence when you question jurors.'

'Don't bother,' said Harris wearily. 'I can recite it to you by heart right now. If a mother finds a jar of jam half empty and then she finds jam all over her kid's face, that's circumstantial evidence and it's as valid as her catching the kid with his hand in the jam jar.'

'Very good,' said O'Brien with mock applause, 'but you did it better in the Cooper case. Are you hitting them hard with the unwritten-law shit?'

'Like a hammer. When I go home weekends, Ursula tells me I even say it in my sleep.' He parroted, in the tones of a reciting child: 'There is no such thing as an unwritten law in American justice. Mrs. Kirschke and Drankhan were engaged in an affair for some time. This evidence may reflect somewhat on the moral standard of the victims. You are, however, to decide on the guilt or innocence of Kirschke and not on the morals of the victims.'

Again the mock applause from O'Brien. 'What's your theory on the composition of the jury?' he asked.

'If my challenges hold out,' Harris replied, 'I'd like to have all women. Women will be sympathetic toward Elaine because, no matter what she'd done, her husband brutalized her. Also, I don't want anybody from Long Beach. They've built Kirschke up down there as a combination Robin Hood and Clarence Darrow. Ramsey, naturally, is trying to get everyone he can from Long Beach, and his strategy is to come up with an all-*male* jury. Men don't like their wives screwing around.'

O'Brien looked searchingly at Harris. 'What do you think of your learned opponent?' he asked.

'The Silver Fox is no clown,' said Harris. 'He does pretty wild things in the courtroom and sometimes I think he took William Jennings Bryan courses in law school, but he's pretty shrewd and resourceful. I hope that later he might go a little far with his dramatics and make mistakes, but right now I don't underestimate him.'

'Good,' said O'Brien. He left and went to his own office.

By the time his secretary, Muriel, arrived at 9 A.M., O'Brien had gone through a mountain of reports on AG cases rang-ing from Sirhan Sirhan's appeal of his conviction for the assassination of Robert Kennedy to fraudulent claims in supermarket advertising. Near the bottom of the pile O'Brien found a note from Eric Collins attached to C.I.I. agent Junell Diemel's report of his investigation of 'Father Robert Nikliborc's activities as Chairman of the Board and President of Boys Town of the Desert, Banning, California.'

Not knowing Diemel as well as he did other agents, such as Frice and Sana, the Chief Deputy was curious about the investigator's style. He judged men by their style. He settled back to read the report and found it thorough, incisive, and fascinating.

Diemel began with an interrogation of Ray Correlo, a former orphan-resident of Boys Town.

> Mr. Correlo was interviewed in private at his residence in Santa Monica. He stated that he worked in the mail room along with several other boys, opening letters containing money and checks contributed by citizens in response to the mail drive. . . . The money was placed in fifty envelopes in a cake pan. . . . Mr. Correlo added that at approximately 2:30 P.M. each day, Father Nikliborc would pick up the money and the bank statement and leave Boys Town of the Desert.
>
> When questioned about the amount of money received, Mr. Correlo stated that during mail drives he counted $700 to $800 each day.

The next subject interviewed by Diemel was Jean Shroyer, a former employee of Boys Town.

> During his first week at Boys Town of the Desert, Mr. Shroyer stated he observed that there were numerous fights between the boys housed there. Also, that the dormitories were filthy, with numerous broken windows. He stated that the meals consisted of small portions of beans or oatmeal and that the medical attention was poor. . . .
>
> In regard to the subject Nikliborc, Mr. Shroyer stated that he began using the name Robert Rand in 1959 and that his identification consisted of major credit cards

issued to him under that name. Also, that Nikliborc took up residence in Palm Springs and began making many trips to Las Vegas.

Mr. Shroyer estimated that $3 million was received at Boys Town of the Desert in response to the mail drives.

Mr. Shroyer stated that this money was solicited to benefit the boys and Boys Town of the Desert only, but that not one 'dime' was expended on the boys for building purposes or for any other necessity mentioned in the solicitations.

Diemel then phoned another ex-employee, Thomas Bormes, who had left Boys Town and was living in Denver, Colorado.

Mr. Bormes stated that on one occasion he observed that a basement at the facility was full of record albums. Also, that a warehouse in Banning was full of doors, and another full of electrical equipment. He stated that he also observed that carloads of food were donated to Boys Town of the Desert. Mr. Bormes stated that this equipment and food were sold by the administrators of Boys Town of the Desert but that none of the money received was ever used to improve conditions at the facility or pay the Brothers' salaries.

When questioned concerning property owned by subject Nikliborc, Mr. Bormes stated that Nikliborc owned a home in Palm Springs and a home in Redlands. He said that the homes were used on occasion for meetings of the Brothers.

Bormes stated that he quit his job at Boys Town of the Desert because of the manner in which donated money and equipment was being accounted for.

Agent Diemel got a written statement from Edward McDonald, who had been a Brother in the Catholic order which administered Boys Town of the Desert.

In his statement, Mr. McDonald stated that during the mail drives all the Brothers, plus many of the children of Boys Town of the Desert, were pressed into service each day counting the money as it came in. He stated that Nikliborc insisted that each day's mail be opened on the day it arrived, even if it would take all night. He added that this rigorous task took place in the basement of the main building. Mr. McDonald stated that many difficulties arose, and students freely admitted that they were taking money and hiding it for their future use. Also, he stated that there were frequent runaways and that Boys Town of the Desert in general was in constant turmoil.

Mr. McDonald stated that Nikliborc would invite the Brothers to his home in Palm Springs to drink and swim in his pool. He stated that he was aware that Nikliborc also had a large ranch near Banning and that he had an airplane and a boat. He stated also that Nikliborc purchased a new Cadillac each year and that he owned four black poodles valued at $600 each. Also, that he was observed to have huge rolls of paper money in his possession which he took particular joy in flashing in front of the Brothers.

Diemel went to Las Vegas to pick up the spoor of Father Nikliborc's alter ego, the supposed heir-playboy Robert Drew Rand. The C.I.I. agent's first interview was with Mrs. Ruth Deskin, assistant publisher of the Las Vegas *Sun*.

Mrs. Deskin stated that she was introduced to Nikliborc by Nancy Fornaseri at the Las Vegas Bowl during a meeting of the bowling team of which she was a member. She stated that Nikliborc was using the name Robert Rand and was introduced to each member of the bowling team by that name.

Mrs. Deskin stated that the bowling team consisted of four other members, including Nancy Fornaseri (who later married Joseph Brletic). She stated that it appeared that Nancy and Nikliborc were close friends because they were together whenever the bowling team would meet. Mrs. Deskin stated that Nikliborc offered to sponsor the bowling team and bought each member a bowling shirt which had printed on the back the person's name and the words, 'Robert Rand Palm Springs, California.'

Mrs. Deskin stated that the bowling team entered the

National Tournament which was held in Denver, Colorado. She stated that Nikliborc financed the entire trip, which began by flying the team to Denver. Upon arriving in Denver, the team was met by a chauffeur-driven Cadillac and taken to the Denver Hilton Hotel. She stated that the team stayed in the best rooms available, with both Nikliborc and Nancy having separate suites.

Mrs. Deskin stated further that the team stayed in Denver for three days and that on one of the evenings Nikliborc invited the team to his suite for dinner. She stated that each of the place settings was decorated with a special cut-glass bud vase purchased by Nikliborc. Also, musicians were hired to play music while they dined. After the dinner Nikliborc gave her and each member of the team an envelope containing a note thanking them for their efforts and a $50 bill. Mrs. Deskin stated that each member also received a bracelet which she later priced at $35. Mrs. Deskin stated that the team then flew back to Las Vegas where Nikliborc continued to support the team for another year.

Diemel sought out other members of the bowling team and they all confirmed Mrs. Deskin's story. One team member Maxine Ruggeroli, added some interesting footnotes:

Mrs. Ruggeroli stated that in 1965 she had gone to Los Angeles on business and, upon arriving, she phoned Nikliborc and he accompanied her to the Beverly Hilton where she stayed for two days with all expenses paid for by Nikliborc. She concluded by stating that she knew Nikliborc as Robert Rand and that she was not aware that he was a Cathloic priest.

The Beverly Hilton Hotel, Los Angeles, records indicate that on March 25, 1965, Nikliborc, under the name Robert D. Rand, obtained a room for three days at $27 a day. He used a Carte Blanche credit card #948 958 571. There were other occasions where he obtained rooms at $50 per day.

Mrs. Ruggeroli added that Nikliborc and Nancy Fornaseri had visited her at her residence on several occasions and that they also went to dinner together several times.

Diemel attempted to interview Nancy, but she proved elusive and would not see him. She now was married to ex-convict Joseph Brletic. Diemel ran a record check on Brletic. The 'rap sheet' showed he had been arrested on charges of rape, first-degree robbery and auto theft, first-degree robbery and jail break. During Nancy's relationship with Nikliborc, Brletic was completing a five-year sentence at the Missouri State Penitentiary for first-degree robbery and jail break. Diemel phoned the penitentiary and discovered that one of Brletic's mail correspondents while he was in jail was Robert D. Rand, 254 North Palm Canyon Drive, Palm Springs, California.

Diemel spoke with Las Vegas casino officials, and they were puzzled about the Nancy-Nikliborc-Brletic relationship after the convict got out of jail. First, Diemel learned, through interviewing Harry Brown, former bar manager at the Flamingo Hotel, how Nikliborc and Nancy had met.

> Mr. Brown stated that Nancy was employed as a cocktail waitress in the Flamingo Hotel casino when she met Nikliborc, who was a patron of the casino. On the first day Nikliborc and Nancy met, he took her to dinner and the next day he bought her a new Ford Thunderbird. Mr. Brown stated that from then on, Nikliborc was a steady customer at the Flamingo Hotel and was constantly seen with Nancy.
>
> Mr. Brown stated that Nikliborc was a big tipper and that most of the bell captains knew him and would go out of their way to help him when he arrived.
>
> Mr. Brown stated that in or about April, 1962, he, his wife, Nancy, and Nikliborc flew to Nikliborc's residence in Palm Springs in a plane owned or chartered by Nikliborc. He stated that they stayed in Palm Springs for several days during which time they played golf at the Indian Wells Golf Course and went to several night clubs, all at Nikliborc's expense. He added that the dinners at Nikliborc's residence were catered. Mr. Brown stated that he observed nothing during his entire friendship with Nikliborc which would indicate that he was a priest.

The matter of ex-convict Joseph Brletic was mentioned with some perplexity by Sam Belkin, casino manager of the Flamingo Hotel, who had given Nancy her job as a cocktail waitress. Diemel wrote in his report:

> Mr. Belkin stated that he knew Nikliborc as Robert Rand and assumed that he was a member of the wealthy Rand family because he was free with his money and had a lot of time to spend in Las Vegas. He stated that it appeared to him that Nancy was playing Nikliborc for his money and that at one point he called Nancy into his office and told her to lay off 'Rand' because he was a good customer and he didn't want to lose him. He stated that it later appeared that Nikliborc was chasing Nancy and wanted to marry her. Mr. Belkin stated that Nancy then apparently married Joseph Brletic and left the Flamingo.
>
> When questioned about Nikliborc's gambling habits, Mr. Belkin stated that in his opinion Nikliborc was a moderate to heavy gambler, He said that Nikliborc would bet into the hundreds of dollars on occasion, but that this was not steady.

Diemel pursued the strange Brletic-Nikliborc relationship further in the Recorder's Office in Las Vegas.

> The recorder's office in Las Vegas shows that on December 12, 1959, Nikliborc purchased a residence at 1605 Bryn Mawr Avenue, a single-story frame and stucco structure consisting of three bedrooms and den. The recorder's office also shows that on January 13, 1964, Nikliborc sold the residence he purchased at 1605 Bryn Mawr Avenue to Joseph and Nancy Brletic.

Diemel then decided to check out Father Nikliborc's real estate deals in the Palm Springs, California, area:

> The Riverside, California, recorder's office shows that on February 9, 1960, Nikliborc purchased a residence at 1194 Vista Vispero Drive, Palm Springs, under the name of Robert D. Rand, a married man. The purchase price of the residence was $49,000. The recorder's office shows a

quitclaim deed from Nancy J. Rand, a married woman, to Robert D. Rand, her husband, dated February 10, 1960.

Investigations into real estate transactions in the Banning area revealed that on January 12, 1961, Nikliborc leased the 190-acre El Retiro Ranch. Mrs. Patricia Jeschke, real estate broker in Banning, was interviewed by reporting agent and stated that she negotiated the lease for Nikliborc which ran for two years at $350 per month. The ranch became known as the Rand Ranch.

The rest of Diemel's report listed such items as Nikliborc's Las Vegas hotel bills, a Robert Rand check for $1,925 made payable to the Flamingo Hotel (presumably to pay off a gambling debt), and the ten cars he owned over a period of five years. Among them were six $7,000 Cadillacs. Two of the Cadillacs were registered in the name of Robert D. Rand, 1605 Bryn Mawr Avenue, Las Vegas, which long since had been the home of Nancy and Joseph Brletic.

Toward the end of Diemel's report was one further provocative note. The C.I.I. agent told of his interview with Robert Berry, assistant casino manager of the Frontier Hotel in Las Vegas:

Berry stated that he talked to Nikliborc when he was a guest at the Frontier Hotel and that Nikliborc introduced his wife, who was a Mexican woman named Cecelia. He stated Nikliborc gambled, making bets in the $50 and $100 range.

The woman introduced to Mr. Berry as his wife was identified by description as Cecelia Gonzalez, a secretary at Boys Town of the Desert. Cecellia Gonzalez is also reported to be Nikliborc's housekeeper.

It was on this note that Charles O'Brien finished reading Diemel's report. The Chief Deputy picked up the phone and called Eric Collins in the AG's San Francisco office. Remembering his Catholic upbringing in Massachusetts, O'Brien said to Collins, 'Nice reading you sent me. What ever happened to poverty and chastity?'

The very British Collins said, 'I wouldn't know about things like that, old boy. I'm Church of England.'

'So I gathered,' O'Brien said sourly. 'Where do we go from here?'

'We have to tie together the money from the Boys Town donations and the money the good father spent on houses ranches, Cadillacs, airplanes, and wine, women, and song.'

'What does the good father say about it?'

'He says that as a successful fund raiser, it was necessary for him to have a nonclerical alter ego.'

'What does the Catholic Archdiocese of San Diego say about it?'

'Not very much. They seem to be bewildered.'

'Weli, the way I see it,' said O'Brien, 'we can either go for fraud on Mr. Nikliborc-Rand, or we might be able to get him on taxes. Let me think about it. I'll call you back.'

As he hung up, O'Brien heard a voice say, 'Don't bother.' The voice was in his office. Miles Rubin, his senior assistant AG, had slipped in while O'Brien still was talking with Collins. Rubin's moustache was twitching, a familiar sign that he either was about to laugh or cry.

'Don't bother to do *what?*' asked O'Brien.

'Don't bother to call Collins back. Matt Byrne, the United States Attorney just phoned me. He got an indictment against Nikliborc this morning in the Federal Grand Jury. Failure to file Federal income tax returns over a three-year period. Money he presumably took out of the Boys Town solicitations and didn't declare. A hundred and twenty thousand dollars' worth.'

O'Brien whistled. For one of the few times in his life, he seemed to be fumbling for words.

Rubin said, 'That's all right. You don't have to come up with a new aphorism. Use the old one.'

'*Which* old one?' snorted O'Brien.

'Only Perry Mason wins 'em all,' said Rubin, his moustache still twitching.

CHAPTER EIGHTEEN

One night, while the Kirschke trial still was in its pre-trial phase, the phone rang in the bar of the Long Beach Yacht Club, around which the tumultuous lives of Jack and Elaine Kirschke and Bill Drankhan had revolved prior to the violent elimination of two-thirds of the triangle. The regular bartender, Jack Sherwood, answered the phone with his usual, 'Hello, Lounge. Jack speaking.'

A voice said, 'Hello, Jack. Jack speaking.' It was Kirschke.

The bartender immediately recognized the voice of the friendly neighborhood District Attorney and said, 'Well, for goodness' sake, Jack, where are you?'

Kirschke said, 'In the pokey, of course.' He then proceeded to chat with Sherwood about the great day he had had in court (it was the afternoon the judge had ruled his arrest was illegal, the key decision which she later reversed). He said to the bartender, 'What do you think of an Oklahoma country boy setting the whole state of California on its ear?'

Harris did not know about this telephone call.

A week later, however, when the pre-trial rulings were mainly going against Kirschke, the phone in the yacht club lounge rang again. This time a part-time painter and part-time bartender named Paul Arsenault answered. It was 7:30 P.M. and in the middle of his pre-dinner cocktail rush. He did *not* recognize Kirschke's voice over all the noise, but the imprisoned District Attorney identified himself. He was angry. He launched into a diatribe against the three Jolly Girls – Pat Katz, Norma McIntire and Marma Herfter – and told Arsenault to get a pencil and write down what he had to say.

Arsenault abandoned the Bloody Mary he was mixing and grabbed a pencil and paper. 'Make sure those three socialites get this message,' Kirschke said. 'Tell them I'm fighting for my life and they better be pretty sure of what they're saying before they repeat anything in court.'

In some manner, Mary Neiswender of the Long Beach *Press-Telegram*, the local Dorothy Kilgallen, enterprisingly got wind of this conversation. She wrote a story about it. The next day Albert Harris sent agent Gene Frice to check out the report with the bartenders. It checked out.

That's how it came about that the tortuous jury-selection process was held up for three hours on the morning of August 31st. Enraged at this new wrinkle in the already unusual trial, the normally imperturbable Judge Parker summoned Harris and Ramsey to a private conference in her chambers behind the courtroom. She reminded the Silver Fox that she had granted Kirschke *pro per* (self-defense) privileges in the county jail only because he was an attorney and assisting in the preparation of his own case. Now, in an abuse of those rights which she thought reprehensible, he was using the jail telephone to make social calls and to intimidate witnesses. Judge Parker stamped angrily back to the bench and announced, 'The former order made by this court is modified to the extent that the defendant will no longer be allowed use of the telephone.' Privately, she told Ramsey that if there were any further capers by Kirschke, he would lose *all* of his self-defense privileges, such as using the jail law library.

The strange interlude had an unusual effect on the course of the trial. The jury-selection process had been going along at a boring, leisurely pace. The prosecution had used up eleven of its twenty challenges, the defense eight, and the judge had dismissed ten prospective jurors for cause (such as opposition to the death penalty). But suddenly, on Friday, September 1st – nineteen days after the proceedings had begun – everyone seemed to want to dispense with the nonsense and get the trial proper under way.

At 2:05 in the afternoon Harris passed on his ninth peremptory challenge and told the judge, 'I am satisfied with the jury as now constituted.' At the time, there was an equal division of six men and six women in the jury box. At 2:40 P.M., when Ramsey had a chance to challenge, he, too, passed and said he was satisfied with the six-six male-female split. The selection of four alternate jurors then proceeded smoothly and without delay.

Before Judge Parker recessed the trial until the following Thursday Harris and Samoian regarded the jury in the same way that professional actors (which in a way they *were*) evaluate an audience before which they are about to perform.

This particular audience, which was to determine whether Jack Kirschke lived or died, consisted of twelve totally heterogeneous people. They were:

George A. Neikirk, a postal clerk for twenty-nine years.

Joe Shelby Piper, a middle-aged employee of the Los Angeles Department of Water and Power.

Sandra P. Almond, a young, attractive Negro girl who was a clerk for the Pacific Telephone Company.

Setsuo Masutoni, also young, a Japanese-American and a draftsman for the City of Los Angeles.

Mrs. Anna Clare Shoemaker, a fifty-three-year-old housewife.

Mrs. Doris M. Wise, a Lockheed Aircraft Company employee.

William L. Brittin, a retired U.S. Navy Chief Petty Officer.

Mrs. Marie E. Chiapel, a stockroom supervisor for a company called Librascope.

Henry J. Kearney, an electrician in his thirties.

Clyde B. Warner, a middle-aged U.S. Post Office worker.

Mrs. Dorothy E. Lawson, a middle-aged housewife.

Mrs. Lucille J. Kinzig, a middle-aged housewife.

Although the panel basically consisted of conservative people with a strong leaning in composition toward housewives and civil service employees, Harris knew, from his intensive questioning of them, that they came from different backgrounds and would react differently to various stimuli. As he studied them, he knew, for example, that his gory photographs of the crime scene would most affect Jurors 2, 8, and 9, and he made a mental note to play directly to them in using such evidence. Jurors 7 and 10, on the other hand, he judged to be methodical-minded and would be the most likely specific targets for his time-schedule and scientific evidence.

'It's a strange relationship and an even stranger game,' Harris told Samoian. 'Here are twelve people with whom we will not be permitted to exchange one word of conversation, yet we will get to know them intimately and they will get to know us intimately over the next few weeks.'

O'Brien was in no mood to indulge in such philosophical musings when Harris returned to the office that afternoon, but he did use a football analogy. 'What's your game-plan after the kickoff on Thursday?' he asked Harris.

'On defense,' said Harris, 'we have to counter their strongest weapon – the alibi, the gas station boys. On offense, the key to our entire attack is the gun, the murder weapon, plus other scientific evidence.'

'And what you're telling me subliminally,' said O'Brien, 'is that we're not too strong either on defense or offense. We can't break the alibi yet, and we don't have the gun.'

'Right,' said Harris, 'but all that might change. In the meantime, we use the old strategy of the punt and the prayer looking for a fumble by the other side.'

C.I.I. agent Gene Frice was not, at the time, thinking of punts or fumbles. He was offense-minded, still looking for the .38 Harrington and Richards Defender, and the frustrations he had suffered were making him angry. Every bit of shrubbery in Naples had been searched for the gun, Navy frogmen had plumbed the murky depths of Naples' waterways, and Frice even had combed the foliage along roadsides leading out of Long Beach toward the eastbound freeways. His examination of state, county, and local police records had turned up nothing new about the gun. Agent-in-charge Keith Byram said to him, 'Why don't you give up?'

Frice said, 'Because I'm pissed off, that's why.' It was not a very profound or even satisfactory explanation, but Byram accepted it.

Frice decided to go back over the entire case, and that night, while his wife Margaret was sewing a dress for their daughter, Robin, he reviewed the thousands of words of notes he had accumulated during the months-long investigation. He came to his interview with David Weinstein, the owner of the United Sporting Goods store which had purchased the gun when the entire model was released by the Federal Postal Inspectors in 1956. He stared at the notes, and one exchange bounced up and saturated his consciousness:

Q: Was the gun in your possession here in the store from 1956 to 1959?
A: No, I sold it to a customer who kept it for a while and then returned it. Then – let me see – some punk held up my store and took the gun. I got it back in a few weeks, though. The police picked up the punk and they returned the H and R to me.

Suddenly Frice knew that this was the mysterious factor that had gnawed on him through all those months of search and even through all his weeks in Alaska. He leaped up, startled Margaret with his hasty departure, and zoomed out of the driveway in his car. He reached the United Sporting Goods Store in Long Beach, twenty-five miles away, just as Weinstein was closing the establishment for the night.

Weinstein didn't remember him, so Frice had to identify himself all over again. Then the agent asked, 'When the gun was stolen from you and returned in 1959, did the police tell you it had been used in any other crime?'

Weinstein scratched his chin. 'Yeah, come to think of it,' he said, 'they told me that the same punk used it in the hold-up of a woman. Shot her in the ass, as I recall.'

'Why didn't you *tell* me that?' said Frice, almost shouting.

'I dunno,' said Weinstein. 'Didn't think it was important, I guess.'

CHAPTER NINETEEN

On Thursday morning, September 7th, the crowds were lined up three-deep and at least a hundred feet down the corridor outside the courtroom, Department 108, where the Kirschke trial proper at last was under way. The baliffs filled the spectators' seats from the head of the line and allowed replacements thereafter only when seats became vacant inside because of defections usually precipitated by boredom. At 11:20 a girl in a yellow sweater emerged and proclaimed loudly that it was nothing like TV. Her replacement, a young man in a khaki bush jacket, said, 'Yeah, but you can't guess how this one comes out.' The line persisted outside the courtroom all day – and on dozens of days yet to come.

The biggest disappointment to the defectors was Harris. After the judge once again said, 'The People against Jack Kirschke,' and Harris replied, 'Ready for the People,' he moved to a rostrum and began his opening argument – after which, as he announced in the beginning of his statement, he would call thirty-eight prosecution witnesses. Only when he was finished with his witnesses, at some indeterminate date far in the future, would Ramsey reply with *his* opening argument and begin the calling of the *defense* witnesses. In the meantime the Silver Fox would be heard only when he chose to cross-examine a prosecution witness. This realization caused groans and immediate defections among some of the spectators, who, conditioned by fictional courtroom drama, could not understand the star of the show being withheld in the wings for so long a period of time.

Harris's opening argument was a scholarly presentation of the facts of the case, illustrated with maps and photographs of the area where the murders had taken place. He told what he intended to prove and went into a lengthy explanation of the motive, means, and opportunity factors in a circumstantial-evidence crime where there were no actual witnesses to the criminal act. The spectators yawned and so did Kirschke, who, as he did throughout the trial, kept popping peppermint Life Savers into his mouth. The jurors, however, were attentive. That was all that concerned Harris. He noticed that Jurors 1, 6, and 11 leaned forward in their seats when he said, 'Mr. Kirschke was bitter, resentful, and jealous. We will show that the bitterness and resentment culminated in the premeditated murder of Mr. Drankhan and Mrs. Kirschke.' Jurors 7 and 10 displayed intense interest when he mentioned that the fatal shots were fired from a Harrington and Richards Defender, which has six lands and grooves in the rifling of its barrel rather than the standard five lands and grooves – and that Kirschke had owned such a rare weapon.

But most significant of all to Harris, *all* members of the jury seemed impressed when he went into a lengthy discourse about a web of lies in which Kirschke seemed to have enmeshed himself. Harris told the jury (and as it later appeared in the transcript):

> We will prove that Mr. Kirschke, when he was questioned in Victorville and in his attorney's office, made a number of false statements and that these false statements evidenced a consciousness of guilt on his part.
>
> We will show that he stated he was in Downey all day on April 7th. We will show he was in fact in Naples at about noon and was observed by a neighbor going into his own apartment.
>
> We will show that while he stated that he knew his wife would not accompany him to Las Vegas over the weekend, he had in fact reserved a room at the Stardust Hotel for Friday and Saturday nights in the name of Mr. and Mrs. Jack Kirschke.
>
> We will show that while he stated he believed Mrs. Kirschke was going to Fort Collins, Colorado, with Mr. Drankhan over the weekend, we will establish that neither Mrs. Kirschke nor Mr. Drankhan intended to go to Colorado because, we will show, they each had a business appointment in Southern California on Saturday. . . .
>
> We will show that while Mr. Kirschke stated that he left the airport between eleven o'clock and midnight, there is evidence that he left the airport no later than 9:56 P.M. . . .
>
> While Mr. Kirschke stated he went directly from the

airport by way of various freeways en route to Las Vegas, there is evidence that he returned to Naples . . . at 11 P.M. . . .

We will show that while Mr. Kirschke stated he registered at the Stardust Hotel at about eight o'clock in the morning, we will prove that he registered no earlier than 9:30 A.M.

We will show that it takes no more than four and a half hours to drive from the Kirschke apartment in Naples in Long Beach to Las Vegas in a 1963 Volkswagen. . . .

Now, as I told you, Mr. Kirschke was asked about the relationship between his wife and the man in whose company she was found when she was killed. . . . He said that his relations with Mr. Drankhan were always quite cordial. He said he had no reason to suspect that something was going on between his wife and Drankhan. He said there were absolutely no hostile feelings among them – that is, between him and Mr. Drankhan, or between him and his wife. He said that his relations with his wife were normal husband-and-wife relationships. And then he refused to answer any further questions on that subject. We will prove that these statements are replete with falsehoods. There was a long-standing affair between Mr. Drankhan and Mrs. Kirschke. . . . Contrary to his statement to the police, Mr. Kirschke knew about this affair between his wife and Mr. Drankhan. As early as January, he asked a private investigator to run a background check on Drankhan, who, he said, was his wife's latest boy friend. . . .

We will prove that Mr. Kirschke's state of mind in relation to his wife and her relations with Mr. Drankhan varied between the jealous and violent conduct observed by neighbors and related by Mr. Kirschke to his secretary, and an attempt to act as if he were indifferent to the fact that his wife was engaged in an affair with another man.

We will prove that on occasions he went to extreme efforts to display a kind of sophisticated indifference, which was, in fact, a mask for jealousy and revenge, which obsessed him. . . .

In order to prove the state of mind of Mrs. Kirschke and her fear of Mr. Kirschke, contrary to what he said, we will prove that Mrs. Kirschke suffered from broken ribs during the Christmas season and told her friends that Jack Kirschke had broken her ribs. . . .

They sat down, the two of them, and discussed their relationship. . . . Eight days after this conversation Mrs. Kirschke was found shot to death in a compromising position in the bedroom of the Kirschke apartment, along with Mr. Drankhan.

Two days after the killing, on the way back from Victorville to Long Beach, the only remorse or concern expressed by Mr. Kirschke over the death of his wife was in the comment, 'I guess there goes my judgeship.'

When he finished his opening argument, which took about an hour, Harris called his first witness. It immediately became obvious that the Deputy Attorney General was going to repeat much of the same presentation he had delivered to the Grand Jury. The witness was James A. Miller, the young Reserve Deputy Sheriff who was visiting his in-laws in the apartment above the Kirschkes' when he peered in through the window of the murder-bedroom and saw the bodies. Harris also led Miller into his now-familiar description of the fights and arguments he had witnessed and heard between Kirschke and Elaine. One of the spectators, an elderly woman doing needlepoint while she listened, murmured complainingly, 'It's the same old stuff. I read it all in the newspapers.'

Harris, unaware of the complaint, stolidly plodded ahead to get all the facts on the record. His questioning of Miller took two days. Then came the testimony of other neighbors and that of Long Beach policemen and criminologists who had been at the murder scene. This consumed more than a week. There was a stir among the spectators when Harris showed the jury photographs of the nude Elaine lying dead in her round bed, but the audience's titillation subsided when it realized, not without some muffled outrage, that the photographs would not be shown to *them*.

It was Ramsey who scored most of the points with the spectators in those first few days of the prosecution's case. Building on his oft-expressed contention that Elaine and Drankhan had been shot through the window by an intruder, he cross-examined young Miller sharply about the window screen that had been removed. The Silver Fox hammered away at the same point in his cross-examination of Long Beach policeman Fred B. Sims, who had been one of the first to arrive at the murder scene. Then, too, he tripped Sims on the matter of the bedroom light which a neighbor had seen go out at 4 A.M., thus fortifying Kirschke's alibi that he was far away at the time, approaching the gas station in Yermo:

Q: Now when you entered the front bedroom of the Kirschke home for the first time on the evening of April 9th, was there an overhead light burning?
A: No. That part of the crime report was a mistake on my part.
Q: Let me read what it says and tell me what the mistake is. 'Officers upon entering the residence noted a red light emitting from the bedroom and upon entering the south bedroom further observed the ceiling light was on.' What part of that is in error?
A: The part about the bedroom light being on. It was the kitchen light, not the bedroom light, that was on.

Ramsey could not shake Sims further, but he had scored. Harris looked worried.

After the luncheon recess Harris attempted to set the record straight in redirect examination of Officer Sims. Much of the case hinged on the state's contention that the ceiling light had *burned* out during the night and had not been *turned off* by some person unknown while Kirschke was miles away in the Volkswagen. Harris questioned Sims as follows:

Q: Did you have your flashlight on, more or less, from the time you entered the front door?
A: Yes.
Q: Now what lights were on in the house when you entered?
A: The light in the radio in the front room, and there was a light on in the kitchen, and also in the bedroom there was a red heating lamp which was on.

Q: And there was no light on in the bedroom where the two bodies were?
A: No. I remember because I had to use my flashlight.

Harris did not know if he had convinced the jury. Juror Number 6 looked skeptical.

The next dramatic exchange between Harris and the Silver Fox took place on Wednesday, September 20th – the thirty-seventh day of the trial. Harris had called, as a prosecution witness, Dr. John Wallace Graham, a physician who had performed the autopsies on Elaine and Drankhan. Dr. Graham, a youngish man with sun-bleached hair who slurred his 'r's' when he spoke, testified on technical matter under Harris's direct examination. He estimated the time of death to be fifty to sixty hours before the bodies were discovered at 10 A.M. on April 10th; he discussed the fact that there was .18 grams-per-centimeter of alcohol in Elaine's blood whereas .15 is the level at which motorists would be arrested for drunk driving; he confirmed that she and Drankhan were in an embrace after just having completed sexual relations, evidence of which was semen on Elaine and around the unzippered fly of Drankhan's trousers.

But the principal information Harris wanted to elicit from Graham was testimony about the direction from which the bullets had been fired. Harris already had made a point to the jury that Kirschke was the only one who knew there was a clear field of fire from the normally unused door between the bedroom and the living room of the murder apartment. Ramsey had made it clear that he was going to contend the shots came from the window, on the other side of the room.

Harris held up a huge blown-up picture of Elaine's head, as it had been photographed in the morgue. There was a gaping bloody hole dead-center in the profile view. Jurors 1, 7, 8, and 9 winced as they looked at it. Harris asked Dr. Graham if he had been able to determine from what distance the death bullet had been fired. The doctor said, 'From more that a foot away, because there were no powder burns.' Harris asked him if he could determine, from the angle at which the bullet had entered Elaine's head, where the fatal shot had originated. 'Yes,' said the doctor, 'from the door near the closet.' Harris asked, 'Could the shots have come from the window at the opposite side of the room?'

'No,' said the doctor.

When the time came for Ramsey to cross-examine, the Silver Fox started slowly. Like all good defense attorneys, he first attempted to impeach the credibility of the witness. Having noted Dr. Graham's youthful and nonacademic appearance, he questioned the doctor about his experience. Dr. Graham said he had graduated from the McGill University Medical School and had interned for a year at the Los Angeles County Hospital. Ramsey asked him about his experience in performing autopsies. Dr. Graham replied that he first performed 420 autopsies at the University of Oregon and at the Sawtelle Veterans Administration Hospital in Los Angeles. 'Did any of those autopsies involve gunshot wounds in the head?' asked Ramsey.

'None,' said Dr. Graham.

Ramsey smiled. 'All right, doctor, tell us where else you have had experience with autopsies.'

Graham said, 'Four hundred for Los Angeles County between 1964 and 1965, forty-five to fifty of which were gunshot wounds in the head and three were homicides. Four hundred autopsies in Baltimore, involving about eighty to a hundred gunshot wounds in the head with about half of them homicides. Since 1966, when I returned to Los Angeles, I have been performing an average of three autopsies a day, for a total of two hundred and fifty to three hundred, with about eighty of them gunshot wounds in the head and about half of them homicidal.'

The Silver Fox rapidly changed the subject.

He sparred for a while with Graham about the phenomenon of lividity – the settling of the blood downward in a body after death – which, Harris and his technical witnesses had maintained, had caused Drankhan to roll off the edge of the bed some time after his demise. Dr. Graham remained unshaken in his belief that this indeed was what happened – that Drankhan rested on his back in the bed for at least two hours after his heart had stopped pumping blood, and then, because of the displaced gravity, had rolled off the bed and come to rest face down on the floor. The blood was accumulated in Drankhan's back, he said. If he had died face down on the floor, the lividity would have concentrated the blood in his abdomen.

Kirschke dozed intermittently during this part of the testimony.

But then Ramsey came up with his first dramatic move of the trial – something everyone had been waiting for – and Kirschke and the somnolents among the spectators awakened.

The defense counsel walked over to a corner of the courtroom, reached into a sack, and drew out two large cherubic rubbery plastic dolls about two feet high. One was marked on its naked abdomen with the medical sign for male and the other with the symbol for female. Ramsey then produced two long knitting needles and asked Dr. Graham to thrust the needles through the dolls' heads at the same angle at which the doctor had said the death bullets had entered the skulls of Elaine and Drankhan. All twelve members of the jury leaned forward in their seats.

Dr. Graham carefully inserted the needles. Holding the dolls so the female was lying to the left and the male doll to the right, as the prosecution had contended the real bodies were at the time of the shooting, the Silver Fox related the position of the dolls to a chart of the bedroom. He asked Graham if he could determine in which direction the heads of the needles pointed. Graham said, 'They point to the wall where the closet and the door to the living room are.'

'But now,' said Ramsey. He paused with dramatic emphasis. He turned the male doll over so it was on top of the female doll in the classic copulating position. 'Now,' he repeated. '*Now*, in which direction does the head of the needle in the male doll's head point?'

Dr. Graham lost his aplomb. 'It *could* be,' he said, 'the area of the open window.'

A murmur ran through the courtroom. One of the spectators, a middle-aged woman in a gray shift, said to her neighbor, 'What an obscene thing to do with cute little dolls,' but her glistening eyes indicated she really was enjoying the show. Several jurors looked at each other and settled back in their seats.

Harris asked for a brief recess and conferred with Samoian. Then, when Ramsey had finished with Dr.

Graham late in the afternoon, the Deputy AG arose for re-direct examination. He walked to the corner of the court-room where evidence and exhibits were kept and picked up Ramsey's two dolls. He flopped them on the counsel table. With the Drankhan doll on top of the doll representing Mrs. Kirschke, Harris said to Dr. Graham, 'Now study this carefully and take as long a time as you want to answer. In which direction would the butt of the needle *actually* point – the needle in the head of the male doll.' Harris held the dolls steadily on the table instead of aloft, as Ramsey had done.

'The ceiling,' Dr. Graham said.

Another murmur went through the room.

Harris then placed the dolls so the heads of the needles *did* point to the window. He resumed his questioning of the doctor:

Q: Does this position of the dolls reflect that Mr. Drankhan's head would have been nearer to the window than Mrs. Kirschke's?
A: Yes.
Q: Would blood spurt immediately from Mr Drankhan's head when he was shot?
A: At a fraction of a second.
Q: Is it not true that no blood was found on the side of the bed near the window, but that blood was found on the side of the bed near the closet and the living-room door.
A: Without a doubt.

That night reporter Sherm Williams wrote in the Long Beach *Press-Telegram:* 'For the first time, the trial, which has moved like slow molasses, appeared to be getting on the road.'

Mixed metaphor or not, the slow molasses got *off* the road again and did not return to it until October 10th – the 58th day of the trial – when Harris called the Jolly Girls as prosecution witnesses. In the meantime there was unexciting but pattern-building testimony from more neighbors, more policemen, Drankhan's widow, Drankhan's other mistress, Elaine's employer, and Margaret Janes, the waitress who had served Elaine and Drankhan their last drinks at the yacht club bar the night they were killed. Two Rotarians testified they had seen Kirschke in Las Vegas much later than 8 A.M., which Kirschke had told the police was his time of arrival the morning after the murder. C.I.I. agent Barney Allen testified that it took him only four hours and thirty-five minutes to drive from Kirschke's home to Las Vegas, allowing for a gas stop in Yermo. Private investigator Joe Carroll admitted to Harris that Kirschke had hired him to check up on Drankhan some weeks before the murders.

But it took the Jolly Girls to fill the corridors outside Department 108 again.

The Jolly Girls arrived, beautifully coiffed and gowned, and under Harris's direct examination, they repeated the same story they had told to the Grand Jury: the facts of the Kirschkes' turbulent marriage, the beatings, the broken ribs, Elaine seeking refuge in the shrubbery outside Pat Katz's house, a bruised Elaine telling Norma McIntire that 'Jack did it,' Elaine telling Marma Herfter that Kirschke had broken her ribs in a fight over Drankhan and, 'I'm just lucky he didn't break my neck.'

However, it was Ramsey's anticipated cross-examination of the Jolly Girls that had drawn the crowd, and the Silver Fox did not disappoint them. In attempting to impeach the ladies as unreliable witnesses, he concentrated his fire on Mrs. McIntire, a small, wealthy champagne blonde whose husband owned a 73-foot racing yacht:

Q: Mrs. McIntire, was one of the activities of the Jolly Girls to cover each other with an excuse in the event one was needed to pacify irate husbands and boy friends and even children?

A: That isn't true.

Q: Isn't it a fact that as a Jolly Girl, you requested Elaine to come to your aid from time to time?

A: No.

Q: Elaine never asked you to cover for her?

A: No.

Q: Was the purpose of the Jolly Girls, first, drinking?

A: There was no purpose. We would take the little boat

and go by the yacht club. It was the bartender there who named us the Jolly Girls.

Q: Didn't you have a way to determine who was the present president of the club?

A: No.

Q: Wasn't it a fact that the president of the club was the person who last engaged in an act of sexual intercourse?

A: That's not true. We had no president.

Q: When Elaine Kirschke acquired the friendship of a flier, did you not then yourself acquire the friendship of a flier?

A: No.

Q: Did you each attempt to have a friend in the same category as the others?

A: No.

This sort of questioning by Ramsey went on for some time, with Harris objecting, and being overruled by the judge, on nearly every question. Finally in the general turmoil, Judge Parker, with a look of perplexity on her face, declared a recess until the next day. The newspaper reporters rushed for the telephones, and the Jolly Girl cross-examination – very little of which touched on the actual facts of the case – got the biggest headlines of the trial in the Long Beach and the Los Angeles press.

The next morning Harris asked for a conference with Ramsey in Judge Parker's chambers. The Deputy AG moved that all of Ramsey's questions relating to the Jolly Girls be stricken from the record because 'they have no conceivable bearing on the credibility of the witnesses.' Harris said, 'Mrs. McIntire's answers were "no," but Mr. Ramsey's *questions* are in the headlines and on television. These are reputations at stake here. I think we should do what we can to see that innocent people are not injured.'

Flustered, Judge Parker said, 'I agree with you, Mr. Harris. I had no idea Mr. Ramsey was going to get into this area, and he took me completely by surprise, as a matter of fact.'

Ramsey argued that he had raised the questions because

the purpose of the *group* was to engage 'in these fun activities.' He said, 'The questions never were intended to show that Mrs. McIntire had engaged in a specific act of impropriety. I didn't accuse her of any.'

The judge said, 'Well, striking the testimony now would be like trying to lock the barn door after the horse had been stolen, or unringing the bell. I feel it is better left alone at this point.'

During the rest of that day's cross-examination, however, Ramsey made only one further fleeting reference to the Jolly Girls. The newspapermen and the spectators were bored again, as the Silver Fox used orthodox questions to try to break down the damaging testimony against Kirschke, and the yacht club women stood resolutely by their stories. Fortunately for the reporters, one incident *did* give them their headline for the next morning. When Mrs. McIntire admitted that she had seen Elaine in the same pink and orange suit both before and after she presumably had spent a night with Drankhan, Ramsey produced the suit and asked Mrs. McIntire to identify it.

At that point Kirschke sobbed.

O'Brien was in the courtroom as a spectator most of the afternoon, and when the trial was recessed for the day, he came up and spoke with the exhausted Harris. 'Nice work,' O'Brien said. 'How do you think you're doing?'

'*Comme çi, comme ça*,' replied Harris. 'Judging from the jurors' faces, we think we're holding Ramsey even, which is the most we can expect at this point. We still haven't used our big weapons.'

'The gun?'

'Yes. And we also may have a little surprise involving the gas station boys.'

Knowing Harris's methodical mind, O'Brien did not press him for the details. Harris would tell him only when he was certain he had something. It was the same with the gun.

Anticipating O'Brien's thoughts, Harris said, 'We're holding off on the gun testimony as long as we can. We probably won't bring it in until the very end of the prosecution's case. Gene Frice is on to a good lead and we're waiting every day for him to run it down.'

O'Brien nodded. He asked, 'What's the best thing going for you so far?'

Harris inclined his head toward the far end of the neighboring counsel table, where Kirschke was just being led away by a bailiff, returning to his jail cell.

O'Brien lifted an eyebrow. 'Kirschke?' he said.

'Yes,' said Harris. 'I've been watching the jury and I'm sure that at least eight of them are shocked at his callousness. Today was the first time he broke down and sobbed a little. Until now he's been looking at photos of his dead wife, nude and with her brains splattered, and there's been the most gruesome testimony, but all he does is looked bored, and sometimes yawns, and keeps popping those goddam Life Savers in his mouth. He acts as though he doesn't give a shit that his wife was killed in the sack with another guy.'

'Why doesn't a smart lawyer like Ramsey do something about his client's attitude?' asked O'Brien.

'Maybe that's his first fumble,' said Harris.

CHAPTER TWENTY

In the meantime work went on for the other members of O'Brien's Los Angeles office. Father Nikliborc, for example, pleaded guilty in Federal Court on two counts of failing to file income tax returns on $119,960. He was sentenced to the maximum term of two years in the Terminal Island Federal Penitentiary, but served only ninety-seven days and was placed on a year's probation by Federal Judge William P. Gray after the priest had undergone psychiatric diagnostic tests in the prison. O'Brien's charitable-trust investigator, John Fiscus, thereupon resumed his investigation to try to find out where the rest of the money had gone. The Archdiocese of San Diego reduced Father Nikliborc to the status of simple parish priest.

Richard Ramsaier and Robert Verstraeten, the heroin peddlers and gun dealers, were prosecuted by the Ventura County District Attorney. Each was found guilty and sentenced to five years in state prison (suspended, but with probation) and with additional sentences to be served in the county jail. Both were safely behind bars, but the Bureau of Narcotic Enforcement agents already were infiltrating the next strand of their dope-pushing web.

Deputy Attorney General Richard Huffman went before the Los Angeles Grand Jury with the case of Beverly Hills attorney Jerome Weber, who had attempted to extract a $35,000 bribe, allegedly for District Attorney's investigators, from murder suspect Thomas Devins. Devins and C.I.I. agents Leroy Sana and Barney Allen testified, and the tape of Devins' conversations with Weber were played in their entirety for the Grand Jury. Huffman also called as witnesses the two DA's investigators, both of whom steadfastly denied any wrongdoing, as in the following exchange between Huffman and the detective who was on the stand:

Q: Now, let me ask you a question as to policy. You have been in the Bureau since 1965. Am I correct in stating that it would be against the policy of the office for the

District Attorney's office to provide any investigative reports to persons outside the District Attorney's office?

A: Yes.

Q: That is, prior to any lawsuit being filed and the matter becoming available by legal discovery?

A: Yes.

Q: Did you ever provide to Mr. Weber or to anyone else copies of investigative reports relating to the investigation of Mr. Devins?

A: Absolutely not.

Q: Did anyone ever ask you to provide a report of that type?

A: No.

Q: Did Mr. Weber ever ask you?

A: No.

Q: In connection with the investigation of Mr. Devins, has Mr. Weber ever offered you money to take any official action?

A: Absolutely not.

Q: Has he ever asked you to stop Mr. Burnett's investigation in any way?

A: No.

Weber was indicted by the Grand Jury. It never was determined how DA's investigator Burnett's confidential report fell into the attorney's hands, or how he knew, within hours, everything Burnett had done and said in his investigation of Devins. Shortly after the Attorney General indicted Weber, the District Attorney indicted Devins for the murder, in Europe, of the still missing Mrs. Norma Wilson.

Gene Frice was digging around in a grave – the dead files at the crime laboratory of the Los Angeles County Sheriff's Department in the Old Civil Service Building on North Spring Street.

After sporting goods store owner David Weinstein had told him, finally, that Jack Kirschke's gun, the Harrington and Richards Defender, serial number 22068, had been used in a 1960 holdup, Frice had spent weeks again researching the local police department files for a record of the crime. Again he had gotten nowhere.

Now, on a hunch, he had gone directly to the crime lab. It was his last resort. Perhaps some local police department had sent the entire file to the lab by mistake.

Frice spoke to Sergeant James L. Montgomery, the senior firearms expert, and Montgomery took him to the dead files in the basement. Frice opened the 1960 file drawer and could scarcely believe what he saw. There it was, the precious missing link he had been searching for for six months. It was a small manila envelope with the following written on it:

LOS ANGELES SHERIFF'S DEPARTMENT R37735.
File No.: RB 273. Complaint: 217 P.C.
Name: WHITE, Toni. Date: 9-22-60.
Gun description: .38 Cal. H & R revolver.
Serial No.: 22068.

The normally placid Frice could not contain his excitement. He went to cross files for Number RB 273 and learned that one James L. Meyer, in an attempted robbery in Inglewood, California, of a girl name Toni White, had shot her in the hip with H & R, serial number 22068, on September 22, 1960. When arrested, Meyer admitted that he had stolen the gun from David Weinstein's United Sporting Goods store in Long Beach.

Frice rushed upstairs with the files. He asked Sergeant Montgomery, 'Did you ever test-fire this gun?'

Montgomery scratched his head as he looked at the files. 'Yeah, I believe I did,' he said. He went to another file drawer and pulled out an envelope. In it were some bullets and a ballistics report.

'Six lands and five grooves?' asked Frice.

'Yep,' said Montgomery.

Frice rushed to a phone and called Harris, who was asleep in his room at the Biltmore Hotel.

Harris said drowsily, 'Did you find the gun?'

'No, but I've got the next-best thing. It was test-fired after a robbery in 1960 and we've got the ballistics. I'm sure Kirschke never dreamed the gun was test-fired before. There was no record of it anywhere except here in the lab.'

By now Harris was fully awake. 'Get Wolfer,' he barked, referring to DeWayne Wolfer, the internationally known criminologist and ballistics expert of the Los Angeles Police Department.

Frice said, 'But I'm sure he's home in bed – like you.'

Harris said, 'I don't care. Ask him to work all night if necessary. I've been stalling this gun testimony for weeks and I've *got* to put it on tomorrow. It's the last day of the prosecution's case.'

Wolfer got out of bed and came to the lab. He made huge photographic blowups of the bullets that had killed Elaine Kirschke and Bill Drankhan, and he matched them with similar huge blowups of the bullet that had lodged in Miss Toni White's buttocks in 1960. He worked all night, tracing the dozens of microscopic striations made on each bullet as it had spun its way through the barrel of the H & R Defender which had fired it.

In the morning Wolfer, sleepy-eyed and rumpled, came to Harris's office. 'Mr. Harris, you're a very lucky man,' he said. 'The bullets all were fired from the same gun.'

Harris said, 'You mean that now we don't have to say that Kirsckhe owned a gun *similar* to the murder weapon but that Kirsckhe owned a gun which was *the* murder weapon.'

'Not a doubt in the world,' said Wolfer.

Harris, Samoian, and Frice all grinned foolishly at each other and then sagged back into their chairs, overcome with relief.

CHAPTER TWENTY-ONE

Great moments in trials frequently come and go unnoticed – except, hopefully, by the jury. In the naval inquiry on which *The Caine Mutiny Court Martial* was based, for example, a series of seemingly unimportant notes and orders written by the ship's commander were much more significant to the trial board than the dramatic emotional breakdown of 'Captain Queeg' on the witness stand. In the trial of Charles Manson and his band of hippies for the ritual murders of actress Sharon Tate and others, a fingerprint of Tex Watson, one of the Manson group, was found at the Tate mansion. It was the first conclusive testimony that the Manson people actually *were* at the scene of the crime. Yet this vital evidence was almost totally disregarded by the press and the public after its orgy of sex-and-mysticism testimony by Linda Kasabian, a Manson defector.

And so it was, too, with Harris's introduction of the Kirschke murder gun testimony. The press, understandably, had just previously been intrigued by the story of the Linda Kasabian of *this* trial – Kirschke's pretty secretary, Sharon Lyle, whom Harris put on the stand as the 'surprise witness' he had deliberately withheld from testifying before the Grand Jury.

Obviously distraught and frequently biting her lip, Miss Lyle confirmed Harris's contention that, far from being placid and indifferent about his wife's indiscretions, Kirschke had reached a crescendo of jealous rage in the period leading up to the murders. She said that Kirschke often discussed his private marital problems with her, 'especially on Monday mornings following the weekend.'

Harris asked Miss Lyle if Kirschke had told her his wife had a boy friend. She said, 'Yes, he did.'

Harris asked, 'Did Mr. Kirschke tell you how he had secured the name of this man?'

'He told me he had beaten Elaine until he had finally gotten her boy friend's name out of her. He told me it was Bill.'

There was much more like this, and Ramsey's cross-examination was lurid, too. The Silver Fox tried to impeach Miss Lyle's testimony as a by-product of unrequited love between her and her boss. She denied having an affair with Kirschke and said that, on the contrary, he had phoned her frequently after work, leaving messages with her daughter for her to meet him at the Stardust Bar in Downey, but that she never had returned the calls. She said Kirschke had developed a rash and blamed it psychologically on her. Miss Lyle did not help Ramsey's cross-examination by volunteering the information that Kirschke was 'extremely nervous, curt, rude, and grouchy to everyone in the office in the two weeks before his wife and Bill Drankhan were murdered.' Ramsey made a brilliant recovery by suggesting to her that 'wasn't it possible that Mr. Kirschke's behavior might be linked to the approaching April 15th income tax deadline?'

It was small wonder, therefore, that after this headline-making testimony ('SECRETARY SPURNED KIRSCHKE, TOO'), the reporters and the spectators settled back for more dull technical intrusions when, at 3:25 P.M. that day, Harris called David Weinstein, the owner of the United Sporting Goods store.

Weinstein traced the history of the Harrington and Richards Defender from the time it came into his possession in 1956. Then police officers told of the other crimes in which it had been involved, and there was testimony about Kirschke's ownership of the gun after he had signed a receipt to take it out of evidence at the conclusion of one of his murder trials. The weapon, Harris brought out, was kept by Kirschke – according to his own statements to the police – in a bedside-table drawer in the back bedroom of his apartment. It would have been unlikely, if not impossible, for a random intruder to have found it in this hiding-place without rummaging around and alerting Elaine and Drankhan in the other bedroom.

The spectators still did not know what was coming when Harris called, as witnesses, experts from the Los Angeles County Sheriff's Criminalistics laboratory. The police officers identified various file cards and bullets from the H & R when it was used in James L. Meyer's holdup of a bar in 1960. Then Harris extracted from Deputy Sheriff Howard

Gavin the fact that in the course of the holdup, Meyer had fired the H & R and one bullet had lodged in the buttocks of Mrs. Toni White. The bullet had been extracted from Mrs. White's person and Gavin had been asked by the Inglewood police to test-fire five rounds from the H & R to confirm that the striations on the test bullets matched the striations on the bullet taken from Mrs. White. Using charts and photos, Gavin showed how the ballistics *did* match and led to Meyer's conviction.

Then Harris called DeWayne Wolfer. The self-assured and debonair Wolfer, the Los Angeles' Police Department's top criminologist and ballistics expert, a veteran of hundreds of such trials, strode to the stand with his blown-up photographs. He told how the night before he had matched the 1960 bullets from the Toni White shooting with the bullets that had killed Elaine and Drankhan. Harris barely had to lead him with questions as he pointed out the exact similarity of striations in his photographic blowups of the bullets. In fact, on one occasion Wolfer even expressed annoyance with Harris for interrupting his train of thought. Wolfer concluded his direct testimony with the most positive statement of the trial thus far:

'*No other gun in the world other than Jack Kirschke's could have killed his wife and her lover.*'

Obviously distressed, Ramsey put off his cross-examination of Wolfer until the next morning. But when it came, the cross-examination could not shake the witness, who, as Ramsey found out by his questioning, had taught ballistics in eight colleges and frequently was retained as a consultant by law enforcement agencies all over the world. As he had with Harris, Wolfer smiled indulgently at many of the Silver Fox's questions, as in the following exchange:

Q: Could you have any opinion as to who pulled the trigger?

A: I would have no opinion as to who pulled the trigger. I'm afraid bullets don't reveal this.

Wolfer did repeat, however:

'The gun that fired the sheriff's test bullets also fired the Drankhan and Kirschke bullets – and no other gun in the world.'

Ramsey finished with Wolfer at 10:35 A.M. and at 10:49 Harris rose and said, 'The People of the State of California rest their case.' It was October 25th – the 72nd day of the trial.

Only one astute reporter caught the significance of the Attorney General's final direct testimony. It was Dial Torgerson of the Los Angeles *Times*, who wrote:

> It was perhaps, the most potentially damaging evidence since the Kirschke trial began.
>
> But the defense contends it doesn't matter whose gun was involved – since it claims Kirschke was in another county at the time of the killings.
>
> During Wolfer's testimony, Kirschke's expression was one of apathy and boredom.

CHAPTER TWENTY-TWO

At 11 P.M. on the night Elaine Kirschke and Bill Drankhan were murdered, an attractive Los Angeles divorcee named Vera Judd was at the Los Angeles International Airport with her son, Webster, nicknamed Squeak, who then was three years old. They had gone to the airport with a man named Robert Johnson, whom Mrs. Judd had met in a drugstore. At one point a tall stranger grabbed young Squeak and prevented him from running out into a traffic-clogged street at the terminal.

The stranger said, 'What's your name, son?'

The boy said, 'Squeak. What's *your* name?'

The stranger said, 'Jack.'

Because of this seemingly irrelevant encounter, Mrs. Judd found herself in court, six months later, as Albert Ramsey's first important 'surprise witness,' as the Silver Fox began his case for the defense in The People against Jack Kirschke.

After Harris had rested *his* case at 10:49 that morning, October 25th, Ramsey presented his opening argument to the jury. The Silver Fox disappointed the spectators because his statement was just as scholarly and unexciting as Harris's opening argument had been. There were no histrionics or quotations from the Bible and the classics. He simply stated he was going to prove that Kirschke was nowhere near his apartment at the time of the murders, that Kirschke was *not* upset or jealously obsessed by his wife's 'adult life as a member of the Long Beach Yacht Club Jolly Girls,' and that his own expert witnesses would contradict the technical testimony rendered by DeWayne Wolfer and others of Harris's parade of police criminologists.

Earlier that day, in moving for an acquittal – which Judge Parker had denied – the Silver Fox had attacked the validity of Harris's circumstantial evidence case. Ramsey said:

'A lot of the circumstantial evidence points to Jack Kirschke because he's the wronged husband. No one has testified he ever threatened Drankhan. Quite the contrary, there is testimony he approved of the affair, he thought of it as an adult arrangement for this lady who had worked so hard these many years. All the circumstantial evidence is as consistent with innocence as it is with guilt.'

In his opening argument, Ramsey promised to emphasize this point, too, as his case developed.

But first he began with his witnesses to support Kirschke's all-important alibi contention. That's how it came about that Mrs. Vera Judd found herself in the newspaper headlines that evening. From his photographs in the newspapers, she had recognized Jack Kirschke as the tall stranger who had prevented her son, Squeak, from running out into the street at the airport.

The incident was important because she set the time at 11 P.M.

At 11 P.M. on the night of the murder, the prosecution had said, Kirschke was home at his apartment, arguing with Elaine and Drankhan, after having left the airport – according to the time stamped on a parking lot ticket – at 9:56 P.M.

Under Ramsey's questioning, Mrs. Judd told a rambling story of the encounter with the tall stranger, and without being asked, pointed out Kirschke, sitting in the courtroom, as the man. She said she had met him after having had a soft drink at the lower-level refreshment stand in the TWA-Bonanza air-line terminal. She was positive the tall stranger was Kirschke.

Taken unawares by the unexpected appearance of Mrs. Judd, Harris sparred with Mrs. Judd for a while about the Robert Johnson who had taken her to the airport. Johnson could not confirm her story, she said, because she found out he was married and had not seen him again. Besides, she wasn't even sure Robert Johnson was his real name, since he might have given her a pseudonym because of his marital status.

Harris tried to elicit from Mrs. Judd some description of the 'tall stranger' she now had identified as Kirschke:

Q: What was he wearing?

A: The only thing I notice about strangers when I talk to them are their teeth. I have dentures and I'm very conscious of it. I always notice if people wear dentures.

He had all his teeth, as near as I could tell. He had a nice smile.

Q: So you recognized Mr. Kirschke months later by his smile?

A: Yes. I saw a picture of him in the newspaper and he was smiling. In the middle of the night I suddenly remembered where I had seen him before.

Q: Was it his teeth that caused you to identify him as the man you saw at the airport earlier?

A: Well, at the moment I didn't think anything about it. I just looked at the picture and threw it aside. In the middle of the night I got up and then it came to me that that was him.

Q: So it came to you like a vision in the middle of the night?

A: Well, I don't know as I would phrase it that way.

Since it was close to adjournment time, Harris broke off his cross-examination of Mrs. Judd and dispatched agent Gene Frice to interview her at home and find out more about her. Frice took DA's investigator Earl Cludy with him.

The next morning Ramsey arose in court in a fury and demanded that warrants be issued for the arrest of Frice and Cludy for contempt of court 'for rousting and intimidating my witness and attempting to get her to change her story.' Judge Parker called Frice and Cludy into her chambers. The agents said that it was a routine interrogation and furnished interrogation reports of the interview. The only unusual thing about the visit to Mrs. Judd's house, they said, was that Squeak, now four years old, had removed the doorknob, necessitating Cludy's climbing out of a window. Also, the child had performed other indignities on the agents, such as biting Cludy on the arm. 'The boy has very good teeth,' Cludy told the judge, 'and I have the marks to prove it.'

Judge Parker also questioned Mrs. Judd. The judge then ruled against the Silver Fox's motion for the arrest of the investigators, saying, 'If *anyone* was harassed, it apparently was the investigators – one of whom was bitten, pummeled, and covered with a blanket by Squeak during the course of the interview.'

The trial resumed and Ramsey surprised everyone with the speed of his defense presentation. Unlike the slow methodical Harris, who kept certain prosecution witnesses on the stand for days, the Silver Fox went through as many as nine of his defense witnesses in a *single* day. The jury seemed impressed with what may have been a release from mid-trial boredom for them. Ramsey called each witness, asked only a few pertinent questions, and then turned the individual over to Harris for cross-examination.

Ramsey scored with two witnesses in particular. One was Jack Ferra, a bartender at the airport, who testified he served Kirschke 'three or four drinks between 8:30 and 11:30 P.M.' on the night of the murder. Again, this was a challenge to the prosecution's contention – supported by witnesses – that Kirschke had left the airport at 9:56 P.M. and was home arguing with Elaine and Drankhan at about 11 P.M.

In his cross-examination, Harris asked Ferra how he could remember Kirschke among the hundreds of patrons he must have served that night. Ferra replied, 'Being a sun-worshiper myself, I noticed he had a very dark tan.'

Next, Ramsey called Mrs. Betty Jean Peterson, who had been a waitress in Denny's Restaurant in San Bernardino, California, which is seventy-five miles from Naples on the freeway to Las Vegas. Denny's is a chain of short-order restaurants catering mostly to the transient highway trade. Mrs. Peterson testified that she distinctly remembered Kirschke as a customer in the San Bernardino Denny's between 12:30 and 2 A.M. on the night of the murders. This was the time, according to the prosecution case presented by Harris, when Kirschke, after having lain in wait in his apartment following his argument with Elaine and Drankhan, shot them in their lovers' embrace when they returned from the Long Beach Yacht Club shortly after 1 A.M. and copulated.

Harris cross-examined Mrs. Peterson and again asked how she could so vividly remember one customer among the scores who flow through a Denny's in any given hour. She replied 'Because he had sausages and wheat toast. That was very unusual. On our menu it was two side orders.' Harris may have partially neutralized her testimony by reminding her that Kirschke had visited the San Bernardino Denny's a week after the murders. Mrs. Peterson admitted that the Assistant DA might have refreshed her memory about his having been in the restaurant and when.

Nevertheless, the Silver Fox now had presented three people who had supported, at least in part, Kirschke's alibi that he was far from the scene of the murders when they had occurred. And the Silver Fox still had his two *key* witnesses to the alibi, the Yermo gas station boys. The defense counsel got to them quickly, on October 27th, the second day of the case for the defense and the 74th day since the trial had begun.

Blond, nervous, All-American boy, nineteen-year-old Dennis Baily came first.

Ramsey established that Baily was cleaning the men's rest room at the gas station early in the morning of April 8th, and then the Silver Fox got right to the heart of the matter:

Q: While you were in the men's rest room, did anyone come in there?
A: Yes.
Q: And who was that?
A: Jack Kirschke.
Q: Do you see him in the courtroom?
A: Yes, I do.
Q: Where is he?
A: Right there.
Q: The gentleman there at the end; is that right?
A: Yes.
MR. RAMSEY: May the record reflect that he does indicate the defendant, Your Honor?
JUDGE PARKER: The record may so indicate.
Q: About what time do you place it when Jack Kirschke came into that rest room?
A: Oh, I'd say between 2:30 and 3:30.

Once again, nearly all the jurors were leaning forward in their chairs. Ramsey then began to question Baily about how he remembered Kirschke's car so distinctly:

Q: When you were finished putting gas in, did you then put the hood down?

A: Yes.
Q: Did you notice anything unusual about any part of the hood, or anything connected with it?
A: Yes, I did. The front license plate wasn't secured on the bottom. It was just fastened to the top, and when you shut the hood, it would catch the license plate and raise it up, and you had to hold the license plate down in order to shut the hood.
Q: Now, when you were holding that license plate, did you notice anything about the front bumper of that car?
A: Yes, sir. It was badly rusted.
Q: How long have you worked, over what period of years, around service stations?
A: I started working for Standard when I was a sophomore in high school, and I still am.
Q: How old were you then?
A: Sixteen.
Q: In your years of experience in the service station business, have you seen a lot of Volkswagens?
A: Quite a few.
Q: Did the rust on this bumper strike you as being unusual?
A: Yes, it did.
Q: And in what way?
A: Well, you don't see Volkswagens with rusty bumpers. Usually they are pretty well taken care of.
Q: Did you notice the paint job on this Volkswagen that you serviced?
A: It wasn't much of a paint job. It was badly oxidized.
Q: Did that strike you as being unusual at all?
A: Yes, it did. You don't – for a VW, very seldom do you see a VW with that paint oxidized on it, because VW's are painted with the same paint as Cadillacs are. . . .

Having established Baily's exact identification of Kirschke's car, Ramsey led young Baily into testimony about the visit to him, a week after the murders, by Sergeant Robert Castillo of the Long Beach Police Department. Baily said Castillo had shown him a photograph of

Kirschke and he had identified the picture as that of the man who had been in the gas station the night of the murders. Then:

Q: Some time later on your shift did you see someone or something else connected with this matter – a car, for instance?
A: Yes. I seen Mr. Kirschke's car pulling in the driveway. . . .
Q: Did you see someone get out of the car?
A: Yes. Mr. Kirschke and a private investigator.
Q: When you say 'Mr. Kirschke,' do you refer to someone here in this courtroom?
A: Yes.
Q: Who is that?
A: Mr. Kirschke. Right over there. (Indicating.)

Ramsey looked pleased. He said to Baily, 'Mr. Harris is going to ask you some questions, so speak up loud, will you?' He said to Harris, 'You may cross-examine.' Harris looked grim. He knew this was one of the crucial moments of the case.

Harris asked a few preliminary questions and then began his counterattack:

Q: About how many cars come into that gas station out in Yermo on a Friday night?
A: Four to five hundred.
Q: So this man that came into the washroom, the men's room, whatever it was, he was one of about four or five hundred cars that night. Is that correct?
A: Yes.
Q: Now, Dennis, how do you fix the time that you saw this man in the rest room, and you filled up his tank, and he went on his way, wherever he was going?
A: Well, I remember there were these girls that pulled in and they wanted their car filled up, so I filled up their car, and they asked for the time and I asked Gene for the time. He told me it was 1:45.
Q: He told you it was 1:45?
A: Yes.

Q: What does this have to do with the man who came into the rest room?
A: Because after that Gene and I sat around, maybe smoked a few cigarettes, and talked, waited on a few cars that came in, and then I started cleaning the rest rooms.
Q: Now, isn't it true that you told Sergeant Castillo that there had been some twenty cars after this car came in with the girls in it?
A: It could be. I don't remember.
Q: And you had smoked some cigarettes?
A: Yes.
Q: Then the red Volkswagen came in; is that correct?
A: Yes.
Q: And isn't it true that the girls came in in their car at 1:15 rather than 1:45?
A: No, 1:45.

Harris produced a transcript of Baily's testimony before the Grand Jury and asked the youth to read page 235, lines 19 through 23. In the Grand Jury, in June, Harris had asked, 'You have a vivid recollection of the girls coming in at 1:15?' Baily had replied, 'Yes, I do.' Harris had asked, 'Looking at the clock, 1:15 A.M.?' Baily had said, 'Yes.'

After reading this section of the Grand Jury transcript aloud, Harris continued:

Q: Do you remember being asked the questions that I have just read to you?
A: I don't remember them, but I remember them when you repeat them to me.
Q: Now, isn't it true, Dennis, that you cannot give a definite time that you saw that man in the rest room and serviced his car?
A: I can give a denifite time.
Q: Weren't you interviewed by a Mr. Byram, who is an investigator for the State Department of Justice in connection with this case?
A: Well, I don't know.
Q: Well, were you interviewed by a tall man who identified himself as an agent for the Department of Justice of the State of California?

A: Yeah. I have had so many of them I don't know who they are.

Once again, Harris produced the June Grand Jury transcript and directed Baily's attention, this time to page 238, lines 17 through 23. Then Harris read this section of the Grand Jury transcript aloud. He had asked Baily, 'Didn't you tell Mr. Byram that you were not positive of the time that this red Volkswagen was in the service station?' Baily's reply had been, 'He wanted a definite time and I told him I couldn't give him a definite time.'

Q: Dennis, were you asked that question and did you give that answer at the Grand Jury?
A: Yes, I gave that answer.
Q: Did you not testify in the Grand Jury that you told Mr. Byram the time could have been fifteen minutes to a half hour either way; that is, fifteen minutes to a half hour earlier or later than 2:30 or 3:30 A.M.?

Having fixed considerable doubt on Baily's ability to pinpoint specific times – as the young man had done in Ramsey's direct examination – Harris concentrated on Baily's equally positive identification of Kirschke. He got Baily to admit he knew, from Ledet, that two police officers were coming to see him 'to ask you to identify a man because he's wanted for murder.' The two police officers were Sergeant Castillo and another Long Beach detective. They first had talked with Ledet, who told them to come back when Baily would be on duty later. Baily said he had rushed out to meet the two detectives when they arrived: they had a copy of a photograph of Kirschke. Harris went on:

Q: Isn't it true that before you were shown this picture, or a copy thereof, which is People's Exhibit 107, you went up to Sergeant Castillo and you said, 'That man was in here—'
A: No.
Q: —'last Friday night?'
A: No.
Q: Isn't it true that you said that to him?

A: No. How could I identify a man without seeing his picture?
Q: That is an excellent question.

By now both Harris and Baily were perspiring profusely. The Deputy AG moved on to the subject of Baily's positive identification of Kirschke in person – as he had detailed it to Ramsey in his direct examination – when Kirschke drove up to the gas station a few hours after Sergeant Castillo had been there. Baily abruptly asked the judge if he could be excused to go to the bathroom. During the brief recess Ramsey, in one of his few friendly exchanges with the Attorney General's lawyers, smiled wryly at Harris and whispered, 'You've scared the piss out of that boy.'

Baily returned to the witness stand, and Harris reminded him that they had reached the point where Baily and a Highway Patrol officer, Sergeant Owens, were in the well-lighted office of the gas station, and Kirschke had driven up with private investigator Joe Carroll.

Harris reached down onto the counsel table and picked up an oversized calendar. He asked the judge if he could have the calendar marked as an exhibit. Then he ostentatiously circled April 8th, the morning of the Elaine-Drankhan murders. He said, 'And may I take the liberty, Your Honor, of circling April 15th?' Judge Parker nodded, and with his heavy red grease pencil Harris made another large circle around April 15th. He turned back to Baily.

Q: Now, on that day, April 15th, while you were in the office with Sergeant Owens in the early morning hours, and Mr. Kirschke and Mr. Carroll arrived, did you recognize Mr. Kirschke as the man who had been in your gas station a week earlier?
A: No, I did not.
Q: When you looked at him, you did not recognize him at all, did you?
A: No, I didn't.
Q: And didn't you tell Sergeant Owens at that time that you did not recognize him?
A: I did.
Q: Today is October 27th; isn't that correct?

A: Yes.
Q: I will take the liberty of circling that on my calendar. It is something over six months since the night we are concerned about, and you testified here today, you looked around the corner of the bench, and you said that was the man who was in the gasoline station; is that correct?
A: Yes.
Q: And a week after the event, you looked at a man and you didn't recognize him at all; isn't that correct?
A: That's right.
Q: Thank you. No further questions.

The following morning at ten o'clock, Ramsey called Gene Ledet to the witness stand. Ledet identified himself by his full French name, Jean-Pierre Ledet. He was twenty-one years old, as dark haired as his co-worker Dennis Baily was blond, and just as nervous.

On direct examination, Ledet told Ramsey he was emptying trash in the gas station at 2:30 A.M. on the morning of the Kirschke murders when he noticed Dennis Baily servicing an old Volkswagen. He walked over and got into a conversation with the car's owner, Kirschke, about the torn upholstery in the VW's seats. Ledet said he himself owned a 1960 Volkswagen with torn seats and he started a conversation with Kirschke about how easily they tear. He said, 'Mr. Kirschke was in full agreement with me that they tore quite easily.' Then Kirschke reentered his car and drove off.

A week later, Ledet said, he did not recognize Kirschke's photograph when Sergeant Castillo arrived at the gasoline station and showed it to him. He suggested to Castillo that if they came back later, Dennis Baily might be able to identify the photo. He admitted he might have told Baily 'the police just want to ask you some questions about a red Volkswagen.'

Harris picked up this point in his cross-examination:

Q: That's all you told Dennis, and it was before Dennis had any car described to him by Sergeant Castillo, yet he said at that time, 'I'm positive that car was in here,' or words to that effect.

A: Right, sir. Probably from what I had said.
Q: But you had no recollection of the car yourself?
A: No, sir, I didn't wait on the automobile other than having a conversation with Mr. Kirschke.
Q: Now when you saw that photograph on the night of the 15th, it didn't ring any bell with you, is that correct?
A: I did not recall anyone from this photograph.
Q: Isn't it a fact that you saw Mr. Kirschke some time later in the early morning hours of April the 15th?
A: Yes, sir, we did.
Q: And he came to your station?
A: Yes, sir, he did.
Q: And he identified himself?
A: Yes, sir, he did.
Q: And isn't it a fact that you did not recognize him at that time when you saw him in person?
A: I recognized him in the sense that he looked familiar to me.
Q: He looked familiar to you. But did you recognize him as the man who had been in your station on the preceding Friday night?
A: Not until he asked me about the Volkswagen seats.
Q: He looks familiar to you today and he looked familiar to you in the early morning hours of April the 15th; is that correct?
A: Correct, sir.
Q: But as to whether he was the man who was there on the night of April the 7th, the early morning hours of April the 8th, you just plain don't know?
A: I can't swear that it was the same man, but the resemblance is so great that it must have been his twin brother if it was not he.
Q: Can you swear that it was Mr. Kirschke that was in there on the early morning hours of April the 8th?
A: This I cannot.
Q: Can you say even definitely that it was Mr. Kirschke?
A: No, I cannot say definitely.
Q: Now, in connection with the time that the man with the torn upholstery came in, isn't it a fact that you have a very vague recollection about the time?

A: Yes, sir, I do have a rather vague recollection about the time.
Q: And didn't you tell Sergeant Castillo when you talked to him that you couldn't help with the time?
A: Correct. I still can't definitely say it was 2:45. I cannot state it was definitely 2:45 or three o'clock, or whatever it was.
Q: Mr. Ledet, in the early part of June of this year, did you testify before the Grand Jury of this County?
A: Yes, sir, I did.
Q: And you were sworn and under oath, weren't you?
A: Yes.
Q: Isn't it a fact that you testified before the Grand Jury that you could not state positively that Mr. Kirschke was in the gas station in the early morning hours of April the 8th?
A: That's correct.
Q: Thank you. No further questions.

On redirect examination, Ramsey asked Ledet about a taped conversation he had had with the Long Beach Police Department:

Q: At that time did you tell them – I am reading from page 22, line 30 – 'We had a conversation about the upholstery that I'll swear to on 15,000 stacks of Bibles'?
A: That is correct. And I still will.

Harris immediately arose for recross-examination and asked:

Q: Well, Mr. Ledet, will you swear on 15,000 stacks of Bibles or however many you want Bibles, that that conversation was with Jack Kirschke?
A: Like I said before, sir, if it was not Mr. Kirschke, the man was so familiar that it had to be his twin brother.
Q: Now, you testified before the Grand Jury at some length. Did you ever say anything to the effect that if it wasn't Mr. Kirschke it was his twin brother?
A: No, sir.

Q: You didn't, did you?
A: No, sir.

When it was over, there was a mass exhalation of breath by the jury as they sank back in their chairs, much like a movie audience which has just watched the completion of a prolonged Indian massacre on the screen. Kirschke sat staring at them, his peppermint Life Savers forgotten for the moment. Ramsey looked haggard, his skin tones reflecting the attractive silver of his hair.

The next morning O'Brien got to his office early again and dropped by to see Harris. Grinning, the Chief Deputy said, 'You were pretty rough on those kids. In fact, you destroyed them. I *told* Tom we needed a mean son of a bitch on this case.'

Harris glowed at the compliment, but he said wearily, 'I don't like beating up on children, but I *had* to destroy them. It was necessary for the case. Those other alibi witnesses Ramsey dug up, I wasn't prepared for them, and they might have been getting to the jury.'

O'Brien said, 'Well, all you have is nice routine testimony from now on.'

'No,' said Harris, 'the worst is yet in store for those gas station boys.'

'Oh,' said O'Brien, lifting an eyebrow. 'When? In your rebuttal?'

'Yeah,' said Harris. 'I want it to be fresh in the jury's mind when they begin their deliberations.'

CHAPTER TWENTY-THREE

O'Brien returned to his own office after chatting with Harris, and an hour later he found himself sitting in the rubble of one of his most cherished accepted beliefs. His long-nurtured system of insulated microcosms – teams of lawyers and agents operating in cells that can continue to work independently regardless of what is happening to the other microcosms – was in total collapse. In fact, all activity in the Old State Building ground to a halt, except for the cases already in court, such as the Kirschke trial.

The catastrophe began at 9 A.M., when Executive Assistant Tom McDonald came in, ashen-faced and with his red beard in nervous disarray. In his hand McDonald had a copy of the Los Angeles *Free Press*, an underground newspaper, which he just had picked up outside the building. The huge front-page headline was: 'NARCOTICS AGENTS LISTED.' Under the headline was an editorial, which read in part:

> There should be no secret police! In this spirit we are publishing in this issue on page 5 the official personnel roster of agents in the California State Bureau of Narcotics for the cities of Los Angeles, San Francisco, Santa Ana, and San Diego.

On page 5 there was another two-inch headline: 'KNOW YOUR NEIGHBORHOOD NARC,' and under it in alphabetical order were listed the names, classifications, home addresses and telephone numbers of all of O'Brien's secret undercover BNE agents.

The previous issue of the radically oriented *Free Press* had run a confidential memo to O'Brien from Richard Huffman, the AG lawyer in charge of the Organized Crime Unit, but this did not involve disastrous disclosures, and the matter was being investigated routinely.

Now it was no longer routine. It was, as O'Brien bellowed to a hastily called council of war in his office, a matter of the most serious infiltration of the Attorney General's office since it had been formed. 'We've got to face the fact,' O'Brien told Miles Rubin and his other chief advisers, 'that we've got a defector here. The list of agents published by this rag is word for word from our roster, which, as you know, is distributed only to our top level and is so secret that I keep my own copy under lock and key. The only way the *Free Press* could get a roster is by someone here in the office stealing it and giving it to them. That means that everyone is suspect – all of *you*, all of the other lawyers, all the C.I.I. agents, all the narcotics agents, all the secretaries. In other words, we now have a case in our own office, with fifteen hundred suspects.'

O'Brien, angrily ripping open his shirt collar, said, 'Let me review the gravity of this situation. Not only have we blown the covers of all our narcotics agents – which, naturally, we can rebuild – but their lives and the lives of their families are in danger from nuts and militants who now know where they live. A lot of the agents are going to have to move. Not only that, but we don't know what *other* documents our defector, or defectors, have taken. We've got lists of informants against the Mafia, the Black Panthers, and the Minute Men. Those informants would be dead in twenty-four hours if their names ever got out. We've got evidence against public officials. If any of *that* raw material gets into print, the whole system of justice in this country gets blown sky-high.'

'What do we do?' asked Rubin.

'First of all,' said O'Brien, 'we lock up all our files and stop all operations until this thing is solved. I don't care how important the cases are, we can't proceed with them until we seal off the leak. Since the leak is here in Los Angeles and everyone in the Los Angeles office is suspect, we can't even trust our own Los Angeles C.I.I. people, so we're going to bring in one of our best C.I.I. agents from somewhere else in the state. He's going to investigate this entire office the same way he investigates any other case.'

A voice spoke up. 'But this *isn't* just like any other case'. It was Ron George, a slim, dark, aquiline-nosed attorney in his early thirties, the son of a millionaire and a millionaire in his own right, who unaccountably worked hard for his living and was one of the best attorneys in the AG's Civil Section. It was he who had been entrusted with the State's case against the appeal filed by Sirhan Sirhan.

'All right,' O'Brien said to George, 'how does it differ from other cases?'

'Because the First Amendment might be involved here – freedom of the press.'

O'Brien said, 'I'm aware of that, but it's going to be *your* problem to solve. I'm putting *you* on the case – under Miles Rubin.'

'O.K.,' Rubin said to George, 'let's get to work and find ourselves an agent.'

The C.I.I. investigator they came up with was Joseph Martino, of the Attorney General's Sacramento office. Martino arrived by plane later that day. Few people in the Los Angeles office ever had dealt with him before. He turned out to be a suave man in his fifties with wavy gray-black hair and a startling resemblance to the younger George Raft. He was known as 'Dapper Joe' to his associates in the Sacramento C.I.I. bureau.

As Rubin and George soon found out, Martino had an unusual background. He had been a practicing attorney with a law degree from the University of Pennsylvania when he gave up his practice in Easton, Pennsylvania, and joined the FBI as an agent in World War II to work on espionage cases. It was he who had trapped the female spy Velvalee Dickinson, who was convicted by the Federal Government of sending coded messages to Japan hidden in children's dolls. Martino had remained with the FBI in San Francisco until 1952, when he returned to the law. After one year he decided he liked investigative work better and he signed on as an agent in the California Attorney General's C.I.I., rather than return to the FBI's nomadic life, mostly because he favored the California climate. Since then he had been involved in nearly all of the AG's most important cases in Northern California.

It took Martino exactly three hours to decrease the number of suspects in the Los Angeles office from fifteen hundred to fifteen. He did this by concentrating on the lesser of the two purloined documents – the memo written by Dick Huffman to

O'Brien. By questioning secretaries and lawyers throughout the office, he learned that only five copies of the memo had been made and all still were in the office. He obtained all the copies and looked at them. One copy, which had been routed to Senior Assistant Attorney General Gordon Ringer, appeared to Martino to have been tampered with. He sent it to the C.I.I. lab. The report came back saying that microscopic examination revealed the staples had been removed and replaced in the same holes. Also the upper corner of each page had been bent back slightly. Both these factors indicated that the pages of the memo had been taken apart for Xeroxing.

All Xeroxing in the AG's Los Angeles office is done in the mail room.

Martino, Rubin and George moved on the mail room. They interviewed the fifteen exceedingly nervous employees there. Martino learned that a copy of the Bureau of Narcotic Enforcement Roster of Agents had arrived in the mail room for delivery to Miles Rubin. Rubin never had received it.

Martino asked Iris Nachtweih, the legal stenographer in charge of the mail room, if any employees had quit or been fired around the time the roster had arrived and disappeared from the mail room. She said, 'Yes. Two of our mail boys. One was Steven Price and the other was Jerry Reznick.' Martino asked her if either of these two young men ever had been in the office at times other than the normal 8 A.M. to 5 P.M. working schedule. Miss Nachtweih produced a chart on which all employees signed in and out when they reported for work and left for the day. On three successive days Reznick had come in as early as 6:50 A.M. and left as late as 5:55 P.M. These days were at the time when both the Huffman memo and the BNE roster had been in the mail room.

Martino asked Miss Nachtweih what sort of boy Reznick was. She said, 'Kind of a recluse. His only friend was Steven Price. I remember he had some strange ideas. He read the *Free Press* a lot, and he refused to touch any files of our cases that might involve the death penalty. When he quit, he said he was going back to school at UCLA. Price didn't give any reason when *he* quit.'

Martino and Rubin went to see Reznick at his apartment

on Olympic Boulevard in Beverly Hills. The youth, twenty-one years old, was attired in jeans and nothing else. He wore no shirt and his feet were bare. He was tall and thin, with long brown hair and rectangular Ben Franklin eyeglasses. He was sitting at a round table littered with books and papers. The sink in the kitchen was filled with dirty dishes.

Reznick knew Rubin and greeted him with tense joviality. He denied any knowledge of the purloined memorandum and BNE roster.

Martino and Rubin then went to the apartment where Steven Price, Reznick's former co-worker, lived with his mother. Rubin asked the boy why he had left the Attorney General's office and Price said he had been offered a better-paying job at a downtown Los Angeles brokerage house, where he now was working.

Rubin said, 'Level with me, Steve, did you take anything from the mail room before you left?'

'Miles, you know me better than that,' the boy said.

Then Martino took over the questioning. Did Price know anyone who worked for the Los Angeles *Free Press?* No, he didn't. Did he know anyone who ever had dealings with the *Free Press?* Yes, Jerry Reznick. In what way? Jerry had come to him with a copy of the *Free Press* that contained the Huffman-to-O'Brien memorandum. Did Reznick say how the newspaper got the memorandum? Yes, he said he sold it to them for twenty or twenty-five dollars. Did Reznick say anything about anything else? Yes, he mentioned at the time he was in negotiation to sell additional information to the *Free Press.* Was anyone else privy to this conversation? Yes, a friend of Reznick's named Joel Kahn was there.

Martino and Rubin went to see Joel Kahn. Kahn confirmed the Reznick-Price conversation verbatim.

Back at the office, Rubin said to Ron George, 'O.K., we're fine so far, but where do we go from here? We're running into the same freedom-of-the-press issue that came up when Senator Thomas Dodd's staff people Xeroxed his papers and turned them over to Drew Pearson.'

'There's one major difference,' said George.

'What's that?' said Rubin.

'The *Free Press* editors had to know Reznick stole the material from us – they even bragged about it, and yet they *paid* him for it. Why don't we treat this not as a First Amendment issue but simply as a case of receiving stolen property? Even though only twenty or twenty-five dollars was involved, *paying* him makes the difference, like a fence buying hot jewelry.'

'Wait a minute,' said Rubin, 'I think you've got something there. Our state law has two thrusts. First, you've committed a crime by receiving stolen property. Secondly, you've committed a crime by withholding the property from its true owner. Let's remind the *Free Press* lawyers about this *second* part of the law and get the documents back.' Nodding toward Martino, Rubin added, 'I think Joe knows how to sew up the case from that point on.'

The documents were returned the next day by *Free Press* attorney Mitchell Shapiro, who once had worked as a Deputy Attorney General. He seemed worried and confused about Rubin's request for the return of the Xerox of the Huffman memorandum and the BNE roster of agents.

Martino was not confused. He put the documents into his briefcase and flew immediately to Sacramento. Ron George, in the meantime, went to court and got an injunction forbidding the *Free Press* to print any further purloined material from the Attorney General's office.

Martino walked into the vast first-floor crime laboratory in the C.I.I. building in Sacramento and asked for a technician named Spiro Vasos. He found Vasos perched over a microscope in a far corner of the lab.

Martino said, 'Spiro, when I was with the FBI we never could raise fingerprints on paper with the regular iodine compounds because the chemicals destroyed the paper. Didn't you tell me about a new gimmick you've been using?'

'Yeah,' said Vasos. 'It's something called Ninhydrin. Comes in a spray can.'

'How does it work?'

'Well, when you touch a piece of paper, the sweat in your fingers leaves a microscopic invisible layer of salts from the perspiration. When we spray the paper with Ninhydrin, it reacts with the salts and beautiful prints come up in a nice bluish color. Nothing happens to the paper. Great stuff.'

'O.K., then,' said Martino, 'I've got a little job for you to do.' He pulled out the Xeroxed memorandum and the BNE roster. Vasos groaned, in the manner of all technicians, and went to work on the documents.

An hour later he phoned Martino's office and told him to come back to the lab – that he had something. He had raised a total of forty-three latent fingerprints.

There are seven million fingerprints on file in California's C.I.I. lab. This total is second, in the world, only to the FBI's eleven million. Among the C.I.I.'s seven million prints are those of Jerry Reznick, who was fingerprinted when he applied for his mail-boy job with the Attorney General; those of Los Angeles *Free Press* editor Arthur Kunkin, who was fingerprinted when he was arrested in 1965 for failure to appear on traffic warrants; and those of a *Free Press* reporter, Gerald Robert Applebaum, whose byline was used on the BNE roster story, and who was fingerprinted when he was arrested a year earlier for possession of marijuana and amphetamines.

These are the three fingerprint cards that popped up when the C.I.I. technicians searched for prints that would match those latent ones which Vasos had raised on the documents taken from the AG's Los Angeles office.

Seventeen of the latent prints belonged to Reznick. Five were Kunkin's, and twenty-one were Applebaum's.

'Well, I guess that wraps up the case,' Martino told Vasos. He was right. Reznick, Kunkin, and Applebaum all subsequently were indicted and convicted.

It had taken Martino, Rubin, and George exactly four days to reduce the number of suspects from fifteen hundred to one and to develop a case that would stand up in court in today's most sensitive area of jurisprudence – possible infringement of Constitutional guarantees. The Attorney General's Los Angeles office was paralyzed for only those four days, and by the middle of the following week all of O'Brien's microcosms were operating again at full swing.

O'Brien phoned agent Martino in Sacramento and said, 'Beautiful work.'

'Oh, it was nothing,' said Martino. 'It was a pleasure dealing with amateurs for a change.'

CHAPTER TWENTY-FOUR

The Kirschke trial had begun in August, which was almost springlike by Southern California's crazy weather patterns. It had proceeded through October, the hottest month, and now, in November, there was the first rain, harbingering winter.

When it rains in Los Angeles, great billowing clouds, predicted days before as they flow across the empty Pacific, scud in procession from west to east in the skies above the city. The rain is almost continuous until the clouds finally pass. The brightly colored sun-parasol mushrooms of the old ladies give way to sturdy and somber black ones. The freeways are encumbered by traffic 'sigalerts' as months of accumulated grease on the pavement slickens in the rain and cars slide into each other like ocean-bound lemmings that have blundered onto a glacier. Mudslides in the canyons carry jerry-built houses down with them into the brush-covered depths. Parking lot boys, eschewing raincoats as a confession of nonmasculinity, go about their work in soaked-to-the-skin bravado, and they are admitted, by the score, to hospitals as pneumonia patients.

Department 108, the Kirschke trial courtroom, had a damp musty smell from the wet clothing of the spectators as the case entered its twelfth week. The pace of Ramsey's defense presentation had slowed down. The Silver Fox had put on a parade of witnesses to try to prove that Kirschke actually was indifferent to his wife's extramarital sexual adventures, particularly the one with Drankhan, and therefore could not have been overcome with enough sudden obsessive rage to commit murder. This was to counter Harris's damaging testimony from Kirschke's secretary, Sharon Lyle, and others, concerning Kirschke's black mood and aberrant behavior in the two weeks prior to the tragedy. Ramsey got his Kirschke-was-as-cool-as-ever witnesses on and off the stand as quickly as possible.

But now, perhaps stung by Harris's annoyingly self-assured experts, such as autopsy surgeon Dr. John Wallace

Graham and Los Angeles Police Department criminologist DeWayne Wolfer, the Silver Fox brought on scientific experts of his own and he seemed to want to take as much time with them as Harris had with his.

The first of the Silver Fox's experts was a private criminologist named William W. Harper, who had set up the crime lab for the Pasadena Police Department. Under Ramsey's questioning, Harper said he believed the bodies had been moved by 'a third party' at least two hours after death. He testified that Drankhan had not pulled the pink bedspread off the bed with him as he fell but that someone had carefully moved his body onto the floor and then arranged the bedspread over his legs. He said he thought the third party – and, therefore, the murderer – was a woman. Ramsey held the gory bedspread up before the jury and Harper pointed out one bloodstain which he said had the characteristics of the imprint of the heel of a shoe. Ramsey asked:

Q: Is this size of that demarcation consistent with the size of a flat heel of a woman's shoe?
A: It could be from a woman's shoe. I suppose it could, without any doubt.

Ramsey's second expert, Dr. Gerald K. Ridge, buttressed this theory. In fact, Dr. Ridge – the doctor who had performed the autopsies in the Dr. Bernard Finch–Carole Tregoff murder case – went even further in his estimate of how long the 'third party' remained in the Kirschke apartment after the murders. He set the lingering-time at 'up to seven hours,' which definitely would put Kirschke in the clear insofar as his alibi was concerned. Dr. Ridge made his seven-hour estimate of the possible time Drankhan's body was moved by the third party, on the basis of the lividity factor – the settling of the blood by gravity after death – disagreeing completely with the estimate of Dr. Graham, the prosecution's doctor.

Dr. Ridge did not pursue the matter of the so-called woman's heel imprint in the bedspread found on the floor beside Drankhan, but he did undertake to prove the murderer might have been a woman by demonstrating how easy it was for anyone – even a slightly built woman – to flip a body as heavy as Drankhan's off a bed. Ramsey volunteered to be the subject of the demonstration. He lay down on a bench, and by twisting the Silver Fox's ankles against each other, Dr. Ridge effortlessly floored him. Referring to Dr. Graham's assertion for the prosecution that lividity had caused Drankhan's body to *roll* off the bed, Ramsey asked:

Q: Is there any other way Mr. Drankhan's body could have fallen to the floor other than being moved there by a third party?
A: Not unless there was a major earthquake.

Ramsey kept emphasizing this point because, if there *was* a third party in the apartment hours after the murders, the less likelihood there'd be that Kirschke, en route to Las Vegas, was the third party.

Except for getting Harper to admit that he held no college degrees, Harris's cross-examination of Ramsey's expert witnesses was not strong. 'We're saving it for the rebuttal,' he whispered to Samoian.

The defense rested its case on Friday, November 17th, the 95th day since the trial had begun. Jack Kirschke himself did not testify in his own behalf. He was not required to under the United States Constitution and he could be questioned by Harris in cross-examination only if he first was called as a defense witness by Ramsey. The Silver Fox did not do so.

Like all good defense attorneys, Ramsey ended his case with an emotional flourish. His last witness was Kirschke's son, Douglas, who just had graduated from Colorado State University and now was a Marine Corps Second Lieutenant. Young Douglas told how much he loved his father and related incident after incident to prove that his father reacted with jovial unconcern about his mother's amorous straying. He described an occurrence that had taken place in the summer of 1965, when one of the Jolly Girls had come by the apartment in the little whaling boat from her husband's yacht. She pulled up in the canal and shouted, 'Elaine, Elaine, come out and play. I have three cute guys in the whaler.'

According to young Doug, his mother got out of bed, dressed, and went off with her friend and the three men in the whaler. The next morning, Doug said, his mother had told him about the previous night's escapade. 'Dad sat in on that conversation,' the youth testified, 'and laughed it off.'

But Doug also made it clear that he had loved his mother, too. 'The last time I heard her voice,' he sobbed, 'was the night before someone murdered her. She told me she was coming out to Colorado to visit me.'

Harris began his rebuttal on the following Monday, November 20th. He called witnesses to prove that Kirschke had exhibited a violent temper in his office and that he and Elaine were so estranged that they slept in separate bedrooms in the period just before the murder. Then the Deputy AG brought back his star – DeWayne Wolfer.

As the L.A. Police criminologist once again made his cocksure way to the witness stand, Ramsey reddened, even in the part of his silvery-white hair. No one, apparently, had annoyed him as much in all his years of court practice.

Wolfer sat down, crossed his legs, and the look on his face indicated to Harris that he was prepared for him to fire away with anything he had. Harris asked why no shots had been heard by Kirschke's neighbors at around 1:30 A.M., the prosecution's estimated time for the murder. As if he were lecturing a class of backward students, Wolfer demonstrated at length how a bath towel could be used on a gun as an effective silencer. He said that Kirschke could have disposed of the towel, along with the gun.

Harris asked if Wolfer could confirm the state's contention that the death bullets had been fired from the unused door between the Kirschke bedroom and the living room. Wolfe lectured once again with his charts and graphs and said it was impossible for the shots to have come from anywhere else.

Harris asked if Wolfe could prove Drankhan's body rolled off the bed without being moved by 'a third person.' Wolfer said, 'Of course. I'll show you.'

While the jury and the spectators gaped, baliffs brought the round lavender-and-gold death bed into the courtroom and made it up with the bloody bedclothes, just as the police had found it. Then Harris called two additional witnesses to assist in Wolfer's demonstration. They were Ludmila Harrill and Ronnie Skaggs, both police officers with the Long Beach Police Department. Policewoman Harrill said she was five feet five and a half inches tall and weighed 125 pounds, the exact dimensions of Elaine Kirschke. Skaggs was six feet tall and weighed 190 pounds, Drankhan's approximate size.

When they were sworn, Harris arranged Miss Harrill and Skaggs in the bed, both lying in the same postcoital repose position that Elaine and Drankhan had been in when they were shot. Wolfer made sure the positions were accurate by pointing out each bloodstain in the bedding and showing the jury, from photographs, the wounds from which the blood had spurted. The criminologist flitted about the courtroom like a stage director giving directions:

'Just take that pillow? You haven't moved it? Now place your head on his arm. You will have to place your fingers here, your two fingermarks right there. Right. Now your shoulder has to come right up to there. Back just a bit. That's it. Now, the gentleman can roll over on his side . . . '

When Wolfer had Miss Harrill and Skaggs arranged, with considerable embarrassment, in postcoital embrace, he demonstrated once again how bullets coming from the door would cause the bloodstains in the exact places where they had occurred on the bedclothes. Then, from one of the photographs of the crime scene, Wolfer made chalk marks on the floor to indicate the pool of vomit in which Drankhan had been found. After that, more stage directions:

'Now, I'm going to ask the gentleman to just let yourself go, slide off the bed, and see what happens with your arm out.'

Skaggs did so. He hit the floor with a thud, landing face down on the floor in the exact same position as Drankhan's body in the crime-scene photograph. The spectators murmured admiringly as if they *were* watching a stage performance, and the judge had to admonish them. But Wolfer still was playing the stage director:

'That is the position Mr. Drankhan was found in when he landed on the floor. Now, Mr. Skaggs, I don't want you to put your head in the vomit there . . . '

The scene was repeated twice more, once under Harris's direction, once under Ramsey's. Both times, Skaggs fell face down again without deviating more than an inch or two from Drankhan's position. Wolfer pointed out that even the urine stain emitted by Drankhan on the floor was in the correct place – directly alongside Skagg's private parts.

Harris asked Wolfer if the sound of the falling body could account for the two sharp reports which upstairs neighbor Frank Cornell heard at 2:30 A.M. and thought were shots. 'No question,' said Wolfer. 'The first report was when Drankhan's arm hit the door, which the murderer left open, and slammed it closed. The second report was when the body itself hit the floor.'

'Then,' said Harris, 'the shots were *not* fired at 2:30 A.M. but considerably earlier.'

'Without a doubt,' said Wolfer airily.

In his cross-examination Ramsey fared no better with Wolfer than he had the first time, much earlier in the trial. For example:

Q: What is there in this case which is even remotely related to the use of a silencer?

A: I think if I fired a gun in that room without a silencer, everybody down the canal would hear it twice. They live on top of each other there. It's like being in a tunnel, and you would have an echo that would sound for miles.

Also, after pointing out the 'woman's heel mark' discovered by Ramsey's own expert, William Harper:

Q: What does this look like to you?

A: It looks like a configuration of nothing.

And finally, in exasperation:

Q: Let me ask you this. Are you ever wrong?

A: No human being is that perfect. I've been wrong many times, but not in the interpretation of criminal cases with physical evidence.

Once again, Judge Parker had to caution the spectators about what could have been a smattering of applause for Wolfer.

Harris had one other loophole to plug in his rebuttal presentation – the alibi issue. First there was the matter of Vera Judd, who said that Kirschke, whom she recognized by newspaper photographs showing his nice teeth, had been at the airport at 11 P.M. and had saved her son, Squeak, from running out into traffic. Harris put C.I.I. agent Barney Allen on the stand. Allen testified that he had researched every newspaper in California and none had run even a single photograph of Kirschke with exposed teeth, smiling or otherwise.

Also, Mrs. Judd had testified that she met Kirschke at the airport immediately after having a soft drink in the downstairs snack bar in the TWA-Bonanza Terminal. Harris called to the witness stand Jerry Glowienke, assistant manager of the airport's food concessions. Glowienke said there were no soft drinks sold in the TWA-Bonanza lower-level snack bar.

Next, Harris took up the matter of airport bartender Jack Ferra who remembered Kirschke still drinking in the bar after 11 P.M. the night of the murder. Harris called agent Gene Frice, who read from tape-recorded statements made to him by Ferra when he was interviewed two weeks after the murders. At that time Ferra said, 'Kirschke definitely was there before 10 P.M., but I'm uncertain as to just when he left the bar.'

But these were only jabs leading up to the haymaker.

Harris startled the courtroom by saying suddenly, 'I call, on behalf of the People in rebuttal – Marma Herfter.' There was stunned silence as the Jolly Girl re-entered the courtroom weeks after her testimony on October 10th. Mrs. Herfter, resplendent in a yellow dress, took the witness stand, and Harris began:

Q: Mrs. Herfter, you were here with us some time ago.
A: Yes.
Q: Now, I'd like to direct your attention back to June of this year. Were you called before the Grand Jury of this county?

A: Yes.
Q: And at that time did you come up here to the Hall of Justice in Los Angeles?
A: Yes, I did.
Q: Now, before you were called in before the Grand Jury itself, did you wait someplace?
A: Yes, in a little waiting room off the Grand Jury room.
Q: Now among the persons waiting to testify did you encounter two young men from Yermo, California?
A: Yes, I did.
Q: Did you have any conversation with one of those young men?
A: Yes, I did.
Q: Where did that take place?
A: Sitting on the bench in the waiting room.
Q: Now, do you know the name of that young man?
A: It's a French name. Jean Pierre something.
Q: Does the name Ledet refresh your recollection?
A: Yes. Uh-huh.
Q: (After Mr. Ramsey's objection was overruled) Now, did Mr. Ledet say anything to you in connection with his testimony?
A: Yes.
Q: What did he say?
A: He said, 'I don't know what I'm doing here. I was asleep when Kirschke was supposed to have been here.'
Q: Did he say anything further?
A: He said, 'I'm just disgusted to have to come up here and waste time.' That was all.
Q: Thank you. I have no further questions.

Nothing better sums up the atmosphere in the courtroom at that moment than the headline on Long Beach reporter Sherm Williams' trial-coverage story the next morning. The headline was: 'LOW WHISTLE FROM JUROR.'

CHAPTER TWENTY-FIVE

In fiction or on the stage and screen, the long low whistle would have been the last great dramatic highlight of the trial – in effect ending it, since the whistle was emitted by Juror Number 3, Henry J. Kearney, the electrician, who was to emerge as the foreman of the panel.

In real-life trials, however, plot values are never clear-cut. Just as actual courtroom cases begin with dull legal maneuvering, they terminate with dull jockeying for position and a frantic effort on both sides to introduce minor points that might have been forgotten, to emphasize matters that turn out to be inconsequentials, and, above all, to get in the last word.

Anticlimactic chaos thus took over in the last days of the Kirschke trial.

Harris introduced Jolly Girl Pat Katz to confirm what Jolly Girl Marma Herfter had said about what Jean-Pierre Ledet had said about having been asleep when Kirschke was supposed to have been at the Yermo gas station.

Ramsey, in cross-examining Mrs. Katz, tried to get her to admit she had made up the story out of pique against him for reviling the Jolly Girls, but Mrs. Katz said she had no animosity toward the Silver Fox and several months earlier had told the same story to reliable witnesses, whom she named.

Ledet was recalled and admitted he *had* told the Jolly Girls he was asleep, but he said he did so only because they were bothering him with questions and he only wanted 'to get them off my back.'

As a last-minute rebuttal witness, Ramsey called Dr. LeMoyne Snyder, who once worked with mystery writer Erle Stanley Gardner in radio's *The Court of Last Resort*. Criminologist Snyder, however, only managed to confuse the issue by disagreeing with both the prosecution *and* the defense criminologists on several points.

Ramsey recalled Vera Judd, who explained that in her identification of Kirschke 'by his nice teeth' in a newspaper photograph, she had really confused two courtroom pictures of Kirschke; one with his son, Doug, unsmiling, and one with Ramsey, smiling.

Harris did not even bother to rebut this latest testimony from Mrs. Judd. She became, therefore, the last of 122 witnesses to take the stand, and finally, in a quiet, almost inaudible voice, the Silver Fox said, 'The defense rests, Your Honor.'

It was December 7th, the 115th day since the trial had begun.

Summations by Harris and Ramsey started on December 8th and lasted for four days. Boredom now had settled on the courtroom, and both the prosecution and defense counsel had to remind the jury that a man's life was at stake and that they should not worry about getting home in time for Christmas.

Summations are not the clear, concise statements of television drama, but as in this case, mostly rambling, disconnected repetitions of facts that have been drummed into the jury's consciousness dozens of times.

Harris began with:

'Now, this is the stage of the case where in the movies you see a lot of shouting. The great advocates were famous for bringing the jury to tears, the great defense attorneys would bring even the prosecutors to tears in the way they waved their arms and carried on. . . . Our theory is this: The theory of the People is that Jack Kirschke took his revolver, and he shot his wife, and he shot Orville Drankhan, and he killed them. . . . It happened in Jack Kirschke's house, it was Jack Kirschke's gun, it was Jack Kirschke's wife's lover, and we submit he pulled the trigger. We submit it is murder. It is the unlawful killing of a human being with malice aforethought. . . . Who else in the world could have done it?'

The Deputy AG then went into a review of the facts brought out in the case to support his trilogy of motive-means-opportunity. He devoted nearly a half hour to Frice's discovery that the murder weapon previously had been test-fired. He said this was the one mistake made by Kirschke, a man experienced in homicide cases, in setting up his alibi:

'Mr. Kirschke didn't know ballistics tests had been run on bullets fired seven years ago from a pistol he later acquired after a criminal case. He assumed no one would be able to find the death weapon. He knew this as an experienced prosecutor – that unless you can find the gun, there is no way you can prove it was that particular gun that fired the shots. He knew that if the gun was concealed, it couldn't be found. That's why he told investigators after his arrest that he owned two guns, one of them a .38 caliber weapon. He had nothing to worry about, he thought, because he had no idea of the test bullets. It was a serious mistake and a bad mistake. . . .'

Harris devoted an equal amount of time to reminding the jury how he had cast doubt on the veracity of Kirschke's alibi witnesses. He also went into some detail on Kirschke's lack of grief and remorse – the consciousness-of-guilt factor. But the jury had heard it all before and the attention of some of them seemed to wander. The only time Harris stirred them was with a fable about the efficacy of circumstantial evidence. 'Robinson Crusoe,' he said, 'noticed human footprints in the sand on his desert island. That was only circumstantial evidence that another human being was there, but it was as conclusive as if he had seen Friday face to face on the beach.'

Ramsey's final argument got big billing in advance from Mary Neiswender, who wrote:

> Mr. Ramsey is expected to draw a record crowd today. Most of the spectators are expected to be attorneys wanting to see the master in action. 'The Silver Fox is at his best in a closing argument,' his contemporaries claim.

But Miss Neiswender herself was seen yawning as the Silver Fox defended the Kirschke alibi for nearly four hours and emphasized the legal concept of reasonable doubt. He reviewed the testimony of his five alibi witnesses and asked, 'How are you going to kill somebody if you're not even in town?'

The Silver Fox did succeed in riveting the attention of Miss Neiswender and others when he referred to criminologist DeWayne Wolfer as 'a tremendous salesman' who reminded him of the carnival hucksters who took his dimes, when he was a child, at rigged games he couldn't win. 'As nicely as the carnival men took my dimes,' Ramsey told the jury, 'Mr. Wolfer told you how that body got off the bed.'

But the Silver Fox didn't reach the anticipated peak of his prowess until the very end. His voice throbbing, his long fingers playing a silent dirge in the air, Ramsey leaned his saturnine face over the rail of the jury box and told the story, from Chapter 37 of Genesis, of how Jacob was convinced by circumstantial evidence that his beloved son Joseph had been consumed by wild animals and mourned him for thirty years; whereas Joseph actually had been sold into slavery by his jealous brothers after they concocted the circumstantial evidence by soaking Joseph's coat of many colors with goat's blood. The circumstantial evidence in the Kirschke case is even more flimsy, Ramsey intoned, and he went on:

'Jack Kirschke has a son. Doug Kirschke has a father. They are involved in a circumstantial evidence case where a father could lose his son, and the son lose his father on the basis of evidence far less convincing than that which convinced Jacob those many years ago. I am sure, as Jacob loved his son Joseph, Jack Kirschke loves his son Doug. Jacob lost his son for those many years because he was convinced of circumstantial evidence that wasn't trustworthy. Jack Kirschke should not be deprived of his son by evidence much less trustworthy than that which convinced Jacob.'

The Silver Fox sat down, wiping his eyes. Kirschke was crying, too.

Samoian poked Harris and told him to look behind him, at the spectators.

'Yeah,' said Harris, 'there isn't a dry eye in the house.'

Judge Parker delivered her charge to the jury on Thursday, December 14th. She told the jurors they had one of three choices to make. They could acquit Kirschke; find him guilty of murder in the first degree; or find him guilty of murder in the second degree. First degree, she told the jury, is assumed to be deliberate and premeditated, perhaps preceded by the killer's lying in wait. Second degree is slaying with malice aforethought, but without premeditation or watching and waiting for an opportune time to act. The judge did not mention manslaughter. Ramsey later told reporters he had asked the judge not to include manslaughter in her instructions. 'That's a cop-out plea,' the Silver Fox said. 'It's what a jury votes when they think someone is *kind* of guilty. Jack Kirschke is innocent and we want to go for broke.'

The jury retired to deliberate. Five hours later they still were deliberating. They were locked up for the night in a hotel.

The next day – and for four days after that – the courtroom was deserted, except for a bailiff standing guard on the jury room door while the deliberations continued. An occasional curiosity seeker peered in, observed the bailiff reading a newspaper or a paperback book, and left again.

Kirschke waited in his cell in the county jail. Ramsey went back to his Long Beach office to tackle work that had piled up on other cases. Harris and Samoian just hung around their still cluttered command post on the sixth floor of the Old State Building. The first day, O'Brien asked, 'How does it look?' Harris shrugged and said. 'You know juries. Who can even guess?' After that O'Brien left him alone.

On December 18th, the fifth day of the jury's delibertions, Harris suddenly was summoned back to the courtroom. The jury wanted to have part of the testimony reread to them by the court clerk. The section they asked for was a detective's testimony about Kirschke's lack of remorse and questioning about how his wife and Drankhan had died, at the time he was under arrest in Victorville.

'That looks good for us,' O'Brien said.

'I'm not so sure,' Harris replied. 'That testimony also gives a detailed account of Kirschke's alibi, as he told it to the police.'

Harris went back to his command post and waited some more. He spent most of his time staring out the window at the visible manifestations of the peculiar Los Angeles Christmas season. There were Mexican-American Santa Clauses ringing their bells in the street, and the avenues and buildings were festooned with white and pastel-pink Christmas trees. The pink and white artificial trees, accentuated by an occasional baby-blue one, glistened in the warm 70-degree sunlight that had followed the spell of

November rain. 'Why can't they have a goddam real *green* Christmas tree somewhere in this town?' Harris growled to Samoian.

At 12:03 P.M. on Tuesday, December 19th – the sixth day of the Kirschke jury's deliberations – a buzzer suddenly sounded on the desk of Judge Parker's bailiff. It buzzed three times. That meant the jury had reached a decision.

The crowds flocked back into the courtroom. Harris rushed over from the Old State Building. Ramsey began the long auto trip from his Long Beach office. Kirschke, in handcuffs, was brought by Sheriff's deputies from the county jail.

There was an expectant persistent hum in Department 10 as everyone waited for Ramsey to arrive. Kirschke sucked Life Savers and scribbled on a long yellow legal pad. He wrote: 'Tuesday, December 19. Weather – white fleecy thunderclouds obscure the sun. Hilltops at Eagle Rock bathed in sunlight. We walk through the tunnel around the morgue. Will it be the last time? In handcuffs, at least? I punch the button for Mr. Gordon's elevator. As I stand facing the door, Joe the bailiff says, "Did they tell you in the jail what they're bringing you in for?" "No." "They reached a verdict. Buzzed at 12:03." '

At 2:05 Ramsey arrived in the courtroom, his briefcase flapping nervously behind him as he slipped in through the door. The bailiff, Joe Postelle, shouted, 'Remain seated and come to order. This court is again in session.'

At 2:12 the jury filed in. They all studiously avoided looking at either the defense or the prosecution tables. At 2:14 Judge Parker entered from her side door and took her place on the bench. She faced the jury and asked, 'Have you reached a decision?'

Henry Kearney arose and said, 'Yes, Your Honor, we have.'

Kirschke wrote on his legal pad, 'Number 3 is foreman.'

There was a half minute of silence so intense that everyone in the courtroom clearly could hear the rustle of the ballots as Judge Parker opened them and looked at each one. She then handed them to Frank Springer, the court clerk.

Springer began to read: 'We find the defendant guilty of murder, a felony, as charged in Count One, and find it to be murder of the first degree, this 19th day of December . . . '

A muted rustle swept through the courtroom. Kirschke swallowed hard and his head slumped forward; his elbows seemed to be attempting to penetrate the hard surface of the counsel table. Harris took a deep breath, and he, too, sagged. He tried to concentrate on the clerk's reading of the guilty verdict on Count Two, the Drankhan murder, but from outside he kept hearing the Mexican-American Santa Clauses ringing their little bells and saying, 'Ho, ho, ho,' under the white and pink and blue Christmas trees.

CHAPTER TWENTY-SIX

'Why do you think Kirschke did it?' asked O'Brien.

He was holding a post-mortem discussion with Harris and Rubin in his office.

Rubin, the house analyst, said, in decidedly nonpsychoanalytic phraseology, 'He flipped. Up until a certain point in his life, he was everything Ramsey said he was – cool, pragmatic, upset about Elaine's screwing around but reconciled to it. He was a big fish in a small pond down there in Long Beach and Downey, and if Elaine's behavior – which wasn't uncommon in that yacht club society – didn't cause any waves in his pond, it was O.K. with him. What he wanted more than anything was that judgeship. All he cared about was that Elaine be discreet so there wouldn't be any bad publicity to louse up his appointment to the bench, which would make him an even bigger fish in his little pond. But then came the Washington's Birthday incident.'

O'Brien said, 'You mean when Drankhan was arrested for drunken flying with Elaine in his plane?'

'Right,' said Rubin. 'It just so happened that they were caught by a police helicopter. This was the first time in history that a drunk flier was nabbed in the air, and as much as they liked Kirschke, the Long Beach and Downey newspapers played it up big. Suddenly Jack considered himself to be a cuckold – in public. He'd go to the Stardust Bar, where he always hung out and was respected, and people would tease him with questions like, "Where's Amelia Earhart tonight?" He must have thought the whole neat little world he had built up for himself was falling apart, and *he* began to fall apart. His secretary and others in his office told us that there was a perceptible change in him, dating specifically from the drunk-flying episode. He brooded a lot, and lost his temper a lot, and that's when he started beating up Elaine regularly.

O'Brien mused, 'Leading to homicidal impulses?'

'Not directly,' said Rubin. 'I don't think he had murder in mind when he left to fly to Vegas that night. In fact, if he hadn't missed the plane, I don't think anything would have happened. But he *did* miss the plane, and he went home, and he found Elaine and Drankhan having a nice intimate dinner-for-two there. The three of them obviously got into an argument of some sort, during which, we know, Kirschke drank most of a whole bottle of vodka. Then Elaine and Drankhan left to go to the yacht club. Kirschke finished off the rest of the bottle of vodka, and then *he* left, too. This is when he probably conceived the idea of coming back to the apartment, getting his Harrington and Richards out of the drawer in the back bedroom, and lying in wait for his wife and her lover to return. He must have flipped completely when he heard what was going on in his own bed.'

'And after the murders?'

'He panicked and ran. He got across the bridge and on the freeway to Vegas. He stopped and got rid of the gun and the towel he probably used as a silencer. He must have thought he'd be picked up by the cops any time. When he got to Vegas and there still was no report of the crime, he must have figured – from his experience as a prosecutor – that he had the perfect alibi.'

'I agree,' said Harris. 'That's why he decided to brazen it out.'

'What would have happened,' asked O'Brien, 'if he had come right out and admitted what he had done?'

'If he had leveled with us,' said Harris, 'and said he had taken just too much, and outrage was his motive, I probably would have agreed to a second-degree murder plea. He might have gotten acquitted or had the charge knocked down to manslaughter, with a minimum sentence, maybe even suspended.'

'And now,' said O'Brien, 'what he has to look forward to is the gas pellets in the green room at San Quentin.'

'Yes,' said Harris. 'Because of his enormous ego, he thought he had the whole thing licked. From the very beginning he was hostile to the police and he was hostile to us. I *still* haven't had one word of face-to-face dialogue with the man.'

'Is there any indication of what swung the jury over to your side in the trial?'

'A couple of them have talked to the press. First, it was

our evidence about the gun, the fact that it was Kirschke's own H and R that fired the bullets. Then it was the collapse of the alibi with the gas station boys. Kirschke's attitude always bothered them – his lack of grief and concern all along the way. The clincher was DeWayne Wolfer and his scientific testimony.'

'Where did Ramsey go wrong?'

'Now that it's all over, let me tell you that if he'd just put on his alibi witnesses and rested his case, he probably would have won. But he and Kirschke were so annoyed by Wolfer that they dragged the thing out by trying to match him with their own criminologists. That's where they fell on their face. And it gave us time to dig up more evidence to break the alibi – and a chance to put Wolfer back on the stand in rebuttal. That bit of Wolfer's with the policewoman and the policeman in the murder bed was a classic. Kirschke's big problem from the start was that he fancied himself the great prosecutor who never could be outwitted by upstarts and novices like us.'

'The human ego,' reflected O'Brien. 'It reminds me of a line in a Josephine Tey book.'

Rubin broke in, smiling impishly. He said, 'Do you mean that after all these years of knocking detective-story fiction, you've found something applicable to real-life law enforcement?'

'For your information,' said O'Brien, not without some indignation, 'Josephine Tey was *not* a detective-story writer. She was a great novelist. She also wrote under her own name, Elizabeth Mackintosh.'

'Forgive me my ignorance,' smiled Rubin. 'What did Miss Tey Mackintosh have to say that applies to Mr. Kirschke?'

'In a great book called *The Franchise Affair*, which I'm sure you've never heard of,' said O'Brien haughtily, 'one of Josephine Tey's characters remarked, "Your true criminal has unvarying characteristics, and it is these characteristics which make him criminal. The major characteristic is monstrous vanity." '

CHAPTER TWENTY-SEVEN

O'Brien and Josephine Tey were proved to be right because there still was one more act to be played out in the Jack Kirschke real-life drama. Under California law, in a murder case, the jury must be reassembled and the same court reconvened for a brief *second* trial – to determine whether the penalty should be death in the gas chamber or life imprisonment. For this second trial Kirschke fired the Silver Fox and elected to act as his own attorney. It was to be the first time he had spoken in court. It also was to be one of the most incredible performances in the history of California jurisprudence.

As in the main trial itself, Harris opened 'for the People.' He could have called witnesses, but he said he would confine himself to a short statement. He said:

'Jack Kirschke is a skilled attorney and a veteran prosecutor who decided somewhere along the line that he was the judge, he was the jury, and he was something else – he was the executioner. When he decided to make himself judge, jury, and executioner, he did something we cannot permit. . . . We submit to you that the evidence we have is not that of an impulsive act. It is nothing less than an execution of two people.'

Harris did not specifically demand the death penalty.

In an almost unbelievable turnabout, however, Kirschke *did.* But first he put on his unprecedented courtroom pyrotechnic display.

He arose, a tall thin man, now gaunt, in a dark suit and sincere skinny black tie. He still had the lanky good looks of a Western movie star, but the eyes now were set deep in his head and the thin lips seemed to be even thinner. What surprised the spectators was the voice, which they were hearing for the first time. They expected the voice to be the low cowpoke rumble of a Gary Cooper, but instead it was high and thin like the exasperated whine of a Don Knotts.

Kirschke, too, called no witnesses. He simply started to talk, as if he were delivering his own closing statement. He began by launching a verbal attack against one of the spectators, a red-haired woman in her sixties, who had been a regular in the gallery since the inception of the trial. Kirschke called the woman 'Madame Defarge.' He explained to the unliterary that in Charles Dickens' novel about the French Revolution, *A Tale of Two Cities*, Madame Defarge was 'a snitch, a betrayer of confidences, an eighteenth-century Sharon Lyle, who sat knitting contentedly, not missing a stitch,' as she watched the guillotine lop off innocent victims' heads.

When Harris objected, Kirschke switched his fire to Henry Kearney, the electrician who was foreman of the jury. He said, 'When I taught night school for nine semesters, there was always one of a particular type of people who always has his hand up. Each time I had a new class, I would check my roll cards and try to figure out which one it would be. And after the jury was sworn in in this case, Mr. Kearney had that hand up and I thought to myself at that time, "Boy! One side or the other of this lawsuit is in bad trouble." '

Next Kirschke insulted Harris by calling him a novice not worthy of carrying Albert Ramsey's briefcase: 'Unless I'm mistaken, it is the first or second for Mr. Harris in this kind of proceeding – off with the old and on with the new.' He said, 'During the process of this trial I was shocked to see those three fine beautiful children of Mr. Harris's in the front row of the press box. Come see Daddy send a man to the gas chamber on the thinnest circumstantial evidence ever in the history of California, and then Mommy will take you out to Disneyland. Isn't that a little bit macabre, Mr. Harris?'

Kirschke became venomous when he reached the subject of DeWayne Wolfer:

'The only marvel to me about Mr. Wolfer is that they don't have him in this Apollo Project to put a man on the moon. With all those talents, with all that great expertise he possesses, they wouldn't be burning up three of our astronauts down at Cape Kennedy, because Wolfer never makes a mistake. And when that aircraft carrier goes out there to pick the capsule out of Atlantic, they won't even have to lower a small boat. Wolfer can walk.'

Much of the rest of Kirschke's discourse was a rambling polemic in which he quoted from the dictionary the meaning of the word 'remorse'; quoted from the Bible about Jesus not testifying in his own behalf before Pilate; quoted from Abraham Lincoln; and quoted from Dial Torgerson of the Los Angeles *Times*. He digressed into lengthy reminiscences of some of his own previous cases. He played throughout with three walnut shells and a pea, indicating that Harris's case against him really was a modern-day version of the old carnival con game. Only occasionally did he return briefly to the relevancies of the proceeding.

There was a recess for lunch, and when the court reconvened, Kirschke leveled all his fire at the jury:

'I care not for what you think. Believe it or not, there are a few other people out there who disagree with your verdict, and they are going to think that when you got down to the nitty-gritty and looked at the question, you blinked – that if you had the courage of your convictions, you would have followed through. . . . If this be construed as throwing down the gauntlet, so be it.'

Samoian whispered to Harris, 'My God, the silly bastard is *challenging* the jury to give him the gas chamber.'

Harris nodded, and whispered back. 'But he's not a silly bastard, he's a *shrewd* bastard. A death-penalty conviction goes directly to the Supreme Court. He's gambling that if he wins on appeal, he'll get out of jail much sooner.'

Kirschke rambled along. He berated two of the lady jurors, both of whom had sniffed when they had handed down the guilty verdict in the main trial, and exhorted them not to waver in their conviction that he should be taken 'into that green room and strapped in the chair and the cyanide pill dropped in the acid.' He concluded by returning to the comparison of his own travails with those of Jesus Christ:

'A Man whose words I spoke to you earlier, who taught all men to live like men, also taught them to die like men, and I promise you, following His precept, to say a prayer for you: "Father, forgive them, for they knew not what they were doing." '

There was a bewildered hush in the courtroom. Harris rose and said, 'The People submit, Your Honor.' Without bothering to get up, Kirschke said, 'Submit it.'

The jury retired to deliberate, and the buzzer again sounded three times, at 2:15 the following afternoon. This time, as the jurors returned, there was no studious avoidance of the counsels' glances, no sniffling by the ladies.

The clerk read the verdict, handed almost angrily by Foreman Kearney to the bailiff:

'The defendant, having been found guilty of murder, a felony, and the degree thereof having been found to be of the first degree, we the jury now fix the penalty as death.'

The strange quiet continued in the courtroom until Judge Parker rapped her gavel and declared the trial to be over. Then the television reporters poured into the room with their cables, chaos, and cameras. Kirschke, ashen-faced until the adjournment of the court, smiled brightly for the cameras – a thin, cynical, hint-of-victory smile.

But the victory, if such it was, was short-lived.

Later, in denying Kirschke's motion for a new trial, Judge Parker commuted his sentence from death to life imprisonment, which Kirschke had insisted would be, for him, far worse than the gas chamber.

In her commutation decision, Judge Parker wrote: 'The Court feels the jury may have been influenced, consciously or unconsciously, by the defendant's argument in the penalty phase.'

CHAPTER TWENTY-EIGHT

Several months later Tom McDonald once again was driving to work down Third Street, and once again he spotted the familiar figure of O'Brien waving futilely at taxicabs outside the Lo-Tel Motel. McDonald stopped and O'Brien went through the familiar motions of lowering himself into the little black Morgan, protesting every inch of the way.

'Did you ever think of *calling* a cab?' McDonald asked.

'I did,' said O'Brien frostily, 'but I couldn't tell which of the taxis that were ignoring me was mine.'

A lot had happened since the last time this little charade had been played out:

Jack Kirschke had successively engaged and disengaged high-powered lawyers such as Melvin Belli and F. Lee Bailey, and now he was busy in his jail cell writing his appeals *himself*.

Attorney Jerome Weber had been tried and convicted of attempting to solicit a bribe from Thomas Devins.

Devins had been tried and convicted of the murder of Mrs. Norma Carty Wilson in Switzerland.

Jerry Reznick, Gerald Applebaum, Art Kunkin, and the Los Angeles *Free Press* all had been tried and convicted of stealing documents from the Attorney General's office.

New cases had piled up in the Attorney General's office, including that of beautiful black-militant Communist Angela Davis, charged with complicity in the hostage-murder of a judge at the Marin County Courthouse in San Rafael, California.

Young Devin O'Brien had recovered completely from the effects of his crushed testicles and was entering a normal puberty, causing O'Brien to observe to his wife, Marie, 'I *told* you it isn't possible to crack the nuts of an O'Brien.'

Thomas Lynch had declined to run for office again, and O'Brien had been the Democratic candidate for Attorney General in the 1970 elections. He lost narrowly to Republican Evelle Younger. In his post-election press conference O'Brien caused mingled sadness and mirth among the reporters – many of whom had covered his activities for twelve years – when one of them asked what he was going to do now, and he replied wistfully, 'I hear the San Francisco Forty-Niners need a substitute place-kicker.' Actually, he was planning to go into private practice and into politics in San Francisco.

For one of the last times, McDonald drove the Morgan into the catacombs of the Old State Building garage, maneuvered around a concrete pillar, and barely made it into his parking place. 'I'm going to miss the daily obstacle course,' said McDonald as they walked toward the elevator.

In their ascent to the sixth floor they passed all the old familiar warrens, peopled by the old familiar faces, working on the old familiar cases. Nearly all of the Department of Justice personnel were Civil Service employees and would remain. Although Miles Rubin and Robert Samoian had gone into private law practice, and McDonald was returning to journalism, the others – including Andrea Ordin, Eric Collins, Leroy Sana, Gene Frice, Albert Harris, John Fiscus, Ron George, all the narcotics agents – were still there, still performing their indict-and-convict missions. Only on the sixth floor itself was there any indication of an impending turnover. A man was politely measuring the offices into which the new Republican upper echelon would move.

'There'll be quite a change around here,' observed McDonald.

'Not much,' said O'Brien. 'For example, guess who was just named to be the prosecutor in the Angela Davis case?'

He threw open the door of Lynch's old office. There, behind a table covered with accordion files – lined up like soldiers, as yet empty but ready to be stuffed with prosecutive information – sat Albert William Harris.

A Selection of Crime Thrillers from Sphere

KISS THE BOSS GOODBYE	Hugh C. Rae	35p
COVER HER FACE	P. D. James	40p
UNNATURAL CAUSES	P. D. James	35p
ASSASSIN	James Anderson	30p
THE ALPHA LIST	James Anderson	35p
ONLY WHEN I LARF	Len Deighton	35p
THE REVENGER: FUNERAL RITES	Joseph Hedges	30p
THE REVENGER: ARMS FOR OBLIVION	Joseph Hedges	30p
THE REVENGER: THE CHINESE COFFIN	Joseph Hedges	35p
THE REVENGER: THE GOLD PLATED HEARSE	Joseph Hedges	40p
THE GETAWAY	Jim Thompson	30p
THE KILLER INSIDE ME	Jim Thompson	30p